Listen More, Laugh Often, Love Always

Listen More, Laugh Often, **Love Always**

Reflections for Today's Church Councils

Dave Wasserman

WIPF & STOCK · Eugene, Oregon

LISTEN MORE, LAUGH OFTEN, LOVE ALWAYS
Reflections for Today's Church Councils

Copyright © 2015 Dave Wasserman. All rights reserved. Except for brief quotations in critical publications or reviews, no part of this book may be reproduced in any manner without prior written permission from the publisher. Write: Permissions, Wipf and Stock Publishers, 199 W. 8th Ave., Suite 3, Eugene, OR 97401.

Wipf & Stock
An Imprint of Wipf and Stock Publishers
199 W. 8th Ave., Suite 3
Eugene, OR 97401

www.wipfandstock.com

ISBN 13: 978-1-4982-0292-3

Manufactured in the U.S.A.

This book is offered to leaders serving today's church councils. It is offered that they may lead and live in Christ's hope for tomorrow. This book is dedicated to those leaders in the Presbyterian community who taught, tolerated, collaborated and worked with me in the four presbyteries I served over twenty-five years (1987–2013). This book is dedicated to my family who lived with all the ups and downs of church service: my children, Matt, Nick, and Kate, and especially my wife, Marney Ault Wasserman, for her encouragement and constant love.

You can't fake listening. It shows.

—RAQUEL WELCH

If you are not allowed to laugh in heaven, I don't want to go there.

—MARTIN LUTHER

Hear, O Israel: "The Lord our God, the Lord is one. Love the Lord your God with all your heart and with all your soul and with all your mind and with all your strength." The second is this: "Love your neighbor as yourself." There is no commandment greater than these."

—JESUS OF NAZARETH

Contents

Foreword by G. Wilson Gunn | vii
Preface | xi
Acknowledgments | xiii
Introduction | xv

1. Grounded in Compassion | 1
2. The Gospel: Being at Peace, Alive, and Hopeful | 4
3. Diversity, Change, Dissension | 6
4. The Shadow Side of the Sexuality Discussion | 9
5. Searching for Ministers | 12
6. Sea Changes for the Church | 16
7. Doing Theology | 20
8. Anxiety, Leadership and Re-Imagining | 24
9. Naming the Challenges | 29
10. Leading Change with Explorers and Benefactors | 34
11. The Church of Christ Uniting | 38
12. Leadership and the Generations | 41
13. Doing Better with Our Disagreements | 45

14	Being Clear	49
15	Education Anyone?	52
16	The Two-Party View of the Church	56
17	Sailing on Choppy Seas	60
18	Anticipating the Next Millennium	63
19	Nurturing Disciples	66
20	A Vision: Discipleship, Leadership, Partnership, Mission	69
21	Editorial: Peace, Unity, Purity	75
22	A Spirituality of Unity	77
23	Editorial: Basic Tenets of the Faith	81
24	The Missional Church	85
25	Editorial: A Different Top Ten	88
26	Editorial: Reclaiming Time to Think	90
27	Editorial: Sermons Are Not Fast Food	93
28	Editorial: Our Witness with Prayer	95
29	Needing One Another	98
30	Editorial: Breaking the Silence	102
31	Faithful Presence	104
32	Listen More. Laugh Often. Love Always.	107
33	A Final Thought: No Whining Allowed/Aloud	109

Appendices

- A Parting Thoughts | 111
- B For Further Reflection | 119

Foreword

I remember a sunny day on a south bound airplane when I could look down and see about half the places I ever lived. The roads, the towns, even the neighborhoods and the memories they invoked. The feelings were still fresh as I looked down on moments of delight, old anxieties, disappointments, and accomplishments remembered in those places. David Wasserman's *Listen More, Laugh Often, Love Always* brings a similar experience as he shares the moments he, in his role as Presbytery leader, put his finger on the pulse of the Presbyterian Church and did his best to recall to it what was really important. Stephen Covey notes the "The main thing is to keep the main thing the main thing." And these reflections are a short history of Presbyterians working together to discern and refocus our energies on that main thing. I too have lived through these moments when the church sought a faithfulness in the midst of tensions which, at the time, we thought might rend the fabric we see God weaving together. I was a youth delegate to the Angela Davis Assembly, a commissioner to the Re-imagining Assembly, an implementer of the PUP report and now continue to remind Presbyterian flavored disciples of the big tent church we are when various anti-diversity puritans (of the right, the left or any other cultural distinguisher) would rather be "aligned" around something other than the main thing. The Presbytery Executive is the primary leader in that regional body who keeps asking that "main thing" question. It is to move the conversation from what "your" main thing is to discerning what God's main thing is here and now. Dave and I walked together in Grace Presbytery for six years together. We honed our understanding of Missional ecclesiology together. We pushed each other across our differences finding each other's hearts on the other side of those moments. We played music together; we sailed together; we have enjoyed the spiritual refreshment of common prayer and single malts together. Indeed I am sure I have given him more material for my retirement roast than he has given me (ask about the time I "insecured" the boat on its mooring). I learned the executive role from him: both what to do and what not to do. He was constantly asking, "What have we learned from this?"—a posture vital to listening, laughing and loving.

I hope you enjoy the flight across our common history working and discerning the Will and the Way of God.

Grace and Peace,
G. Wilson Gunn, Jr.
General Presbyter, National Capital Presbytery
Epiphany, 2015

Preface

I have concluded that history is neither linear nor circular. It is three-dimensional. The image of the spiral comes closest to mind. History has a sense of both repeating itself and yet moving forward. So it is that I think the last quarter-century in the life of the Christian church in the United States can speak to today's church. We have learned some things and are prompted by our gracious God to consider that who we are today is partly a result of the path we have traveled. How did we lead? What did we learn? What might our experiences suggest for leaders called to serve Jesus Christ in this new time and place?

This manuscript was shaped from my years of service in the Presbyterian Church (USA), where I was privileged to observe and lead in several of the mid-councils we call presbyteries. While Presbyterians bring their own ideas and experiences to the church of Jesus Christ, we aren't that unique. I trust there is something in these pages to offer our brothers and sisters who serve in the dioceses, districts, synods, consistories, sessions and other decision-making bodies of the whole community of believers.

The chapters are taken from three sources: (1) verbal reports presented to the presbyteries when they met, (2) written editorials for various presbytery publications, and (3) in the Appendix, three sermons offered for further reflection. Each chapter begins with a brief introduction and concludes with a suggested question or two to help leadership teams engage a conversation.

Preface

I truly believe God's call now is best grounded in our listening more, laughing often, and loving always, even the folks who are hard to love. As Thelma Westbrook, a Tennessee Baptist Sunday School Teacher once told her pupil, Will Campbell, the civil rights activist who was also a chaplain to the Ku Klux Klan: If you just love the people what's easy to love, that really ain't no love at all. If you love one, you have to love 'em all." (from *Brother to a Dragonfly*, Seabury, 1977).

Dave Wasserman
November 2014

Acknowledgments

My thanks to the Presbyterian communities of believers, especially in Michigan, Oklahoma, Texas and Arizona where I served the ruling and teaching elders of the congregations in four presbyteries, mid-councils of our church. For over a quarter century, these good folks listened to, laughed with and loved me along the way. They shared their insights, challenged my thinking, and helped me mature in this work.

Special thanks to dear friends, partners, and colleagues who have shaped what follows in direct and indirect ways. Among them: Bob and Carol Adcock of Fort Worth, Texas; Ed Albright of Atlanta, Georgia; Claire Breihan of Austin, Texas; Phil Brown of Minneapolis, Minnesota; Rick Carus of Willmar, Minnesota; Bob Chapman (deceased) of Scottsdale, Arizona; Earl and Jean Christman (deceased) of Phoenix, Arizona; Greg Coulter of Tulsa, Oklahoma; Bob and Sherry Curry of Tulsa, Oklahoma; Jeff Finch of Belen, New Mexico; Judy and David Fletcher of Carrollton, Texas; Bill Fogleman (deceased) of Wimberly, Texas; Pat Geadelmann of Cedar Falls, Iowa; Wilson Gunn of Washington, DC; Jack Haberer of Naples, Florida; Jill Hudson of Louisville, Kentucky; Ann Lamar of Tulsa, Oklahoma; Bob and Pat Lucy of Tulsa, Oklahoma; Jim Mead of Gig Harbor, Washington; Dick and Karin Miller of Seattle, Washington; Anna Milligan of Tulsa, Oklahoma; John Nelsen of El Paso, Texas; Stan Ott of Vienna, Virginia; Dale Patterson of Irving, Texas; Brad Rohwer of Estes Park, Colorado; Fred and Barbara Ryle of Weatherford, Texas; Joe Small of Louisville,

Acknowledgments

Kentucky; O. R. Schmidt of Austin, Texas; Verne Sindlinger of Nashville, Indiana; Ted and Mary Sperduto of Wausau, Wisconsin; Peter and Donna Sword of Winterville, North Carolina; Sheryl Taylor of Bedford, Texas; Russell TePaske of Cedar Falls, Iowa; Mike Thompson of Arlington, Texas; Ted and Rosie Walkenhorst of Jenkintown, Pennsylvania; Kim and Diana Warner of Argyle, Texas; Sue Westfall of Atlanta, Georgia; Paul and Joyce Williams of Fort Worth, Texas; Gene Horse Wilson of Chickasaw, Oklahoma; Janine Wilson of Marysville, Ohio; and Tom York of Cincinnati, Ohio. These friends are the tip of an iceberg of insight, patience, and encouragement.

Three of them offered comments and suggestions in the development of this manuscript: Ruling Elders Carol Adcock, Ted Walkenhorst, and Kim Warner.

Finally, my deepest thanks goes to Marney, my marriage partner of forty-two years, colleague in ministry, kind wordsmith and best friend.

Introduction

This book is about leadership. It focuses on three sustaining ideas. First, leadership is about asking good questions. Second, leadership is about dialogue and conversation. Finally, leadership is about passion and values.

This book is for leaders . . . for leaders serving at all councils of the church . . . for leaders who want to dialogue and find their way rather than follow someone else's blueprint.

Beginning in the second half of the last century, the fabric of the church began to unravel both as an institution and as an agent of God's mission. Some saw the church being taken hostage by those who were convinced that their solutions alone were God's. Others watched the church wander off its familiar path into an uncharted wilderness. Whether gripped by controversy or lost, God has been calling the church to make deep changes in its orientation, structures and mission engagement. Today, the church continues to face such a season, even as we are gaining some clarity, movement and hope. It is good to remember that all of our life is in God's hands, including this time.

This book is a collection of verbal reports, editorials, and occasional sermons. They are one person's response to this season in our church. While some comments speak to a particular issue in the council where I served, many address the broader challenges and crises across the body of Jesus Christ in our country. All are offered as a prompting for the reader's thinking, conversation, discernment and decision work.

Introduction

Finally this book is intended as a reminder that there is a forest to see beyond the particular trees we engage. Leadership is about that big picture, and helping those we serve remember deeper and broader truths about our God, about the church's history and our contributions to it.

Catholic Bishop Oscar Romero (1917–1980) is credited with these words:

> It helps now and then to step back and take the long view;
> The Kingdom is not only beyond our efforts, it is beyond our vision.
> We accomplish in our lifetime only a tiny fraction
> of the magnificent enterprise that is God's work.
>
> We plant the seeds that one day will grow.
> We water the seeds that are already planted.
> We lay foundations that will need further development.
>
> And there is a sense of liberation in realizing that
> we cannot do everything.
> It may be incomplete, but it is a beginning...
>
> and an opportunity for the Lord's grace to enter and do the rest.
> We may never see the end results
> but that is the difference between the master-builder and the worker.
> We are workers, not master builders; ministers, not messiahs.
>
> We are prophets of a future not our own.

May you find encouragement in these pages as you help lead into a future not our own.

1
Grounded in Compassion

June 1990

My first report as a new executive presbyter was presented to Eastern Oklahoma in June 1990. What do you say to a new community you are serving? I chose the theme of compassion as a starting point. After some words of appreciation for the warm welcome I had received:

Friends: What I want to share for a few moments is a thought about where we might be headed. Perhaps, more accurately, where we might be grounded as we move into God's future.

There is an image of the church's ministry that is becoming increasingly important to me, because I believe that it holds a clue for some of the major dilemmas of the church right now. It is the image of compassion.

It is revealing to note that the two major mission directions of our denomination right now are evangelism and social justice. To set these as our major aims is to acknowledge their importance and to admit, at least to some degree, that we are doing neither one of them very well. I would agree and suggest the reason that both our evangelism and our social justice are failing to bring renewal is because both are no longer grounded in what holds them together:

the fundamental ministry of compassion of one person towards another that forms the center of the Christian life.

The cup of cold water, the kind word, the time taken to encounter the living God in our relationships—however you imagine it—it is compassion that lies at the heart of God's love for this world, of Jesus' ministry on this earth, of the Spirit's dwelling among us. Andrew Purves, professor at Pittsburgh Theological Seminary, begins his newest book by recalling the words of Nicholas Wolterstorff in that man's *Lament for a Son*.

> Please. Don't say it's not really so bad. Because it is. Death is awful, demonic. If you think your task as comforter is to tell me that really, all things considered, it's not so bad, you do not sit with me in my grief but place yourself off in the distance away from me. What I need to hear from you is that you recognize how painful it is. I need to hear from you that you are with me in my desperation. To comfort me, you have to come close. Come sit with me on my mourning bench. (p. 34)

Purves finds in these words his definition of compassion: sitting with someone on his or her mourning bench. It is that kind of presence—sitting on a mourning bench—that is needed and is at the heart of all ministry, whether we encounter a stranger in the name of evangelism or we encounter a stranger in the name of social justice.

I wonder if our being out of touch with the ministry of compassion might begin to explain:

- our membership decline, where we welcome folks in the front door and, in our concern for counting numbers, let them slip out the back unnoticed
- our financial stress, where a person's wealth is too often reduced to dollar signs and doesn't include their ideas and creativity for how to use those dollars
- our frustrations with the distances between the congregation, the mid-councils of our presbyteries and synods, and the General Assembly

- our bickering between such divergent groups as the Presbyterian Lay Committee and the Witherspoon Society, where suspicion and mistrust have eroded the faith that is supposed to hold us together

Since my arrival in May, I have been privileged to observe one session addressing a critical staff issue. I have watched one of our presbytery committees work with a congregation over a difficult decision. There has been genuine wrestling and I have sensed the compassion and love of Christ at work.

All of this suggests that, if our Presbytery would be strong, then the decisions and the ministry and the work and the worship we share needs to be grounded in that compassion where we see in one another other people who are on a journey with God and who would join us in that ever-tenuous task of being faithful to God's calling. Listening, engaging, embracing, responding. Those are critical to the way we do our work and the way we make our decisions.

It is in the central place of compassion that I believe the whole church and all of its parts has its hope. That is my wish for all of us, for our congregations, and Eastern Oklahoma Presbytery. So, how do you see this? I'd welcome your reflections on what we must keep in mind as we move through this day and the coming months.

There is a difference between compassion and empathy. Empathy can be a way to relieve people of their responsibilities. Compassion invites people to claim their lives knowing that there are friends, helpers, fellow journeyers to accompany us. Where do you see true compassion being offered in the ministries of which you participate? In your congregation? In your mid-Council?

2

The Gospel

Being at Peace, Alive, and Hopeful

September 1990

In Eastern Oklahoma Presbytery, the September meeting each year was held at the Dwight Mission Camp near the Arkansas border. They were two day events that included time for worship, business and educational programs and conversations.

Our three program times this weekend include a discussion on evangelism, a Bible study, and a conversation about the life of our presbytery. A comment about the first of these:

The word evangelism comes from the Greek *evangelion*, which means to announce the good news. For some of us, the difficult part of that task is not engaging another person in a conversation, but in finding the right words to express our faith. How do we understand the faith? What is it that God wants for us?

As I read the gospels and reflect on the whole of God's story in Scripture, I am increasingly aware of three ideas, that brought together, answer the question of what God wants for our lives:

- to be at peace with our past
- to be alive to the present
- to be hopeful about the future

Being at peace with the past means to find the balance between trivializing our history and idolizing it. History is not bunk, as Henry Ford once declared. But neither is our history to be the center of our worship, literally or figuratively. Being at peace means finding the balance between letting go of our past mistakes and learning from them. And some of our past may not be mistakes at all but simply appropriate actions for a different time and place. God wants us to be at peace with our past.

God wants us to be alive to the present, too. The image that comes to mind is someone who is aware of what may be going on around him or her, who lives energetically. Being alive to the present means living our answer to my favorite ordination question: will you serve with energy, intelligence, imagination and love?

And no less important is the sense that God wants us to be hopeful about the future. In Jesus Christ, our hope is secured. Through Jesus Christ, the church has dared to announce God's message of hope to a fearful world. Through the message of the gospel, God is inviting us to be hopeful and to live in that hope.

In worship each week, Christians move through these three as the liturgy takes us from confession through proclamation to benediction. And, this three-legged way of engaging the gospel has as much to say about life in a presbytery. Consider then, just how God is inviting us to be at peace with our past, alive to the present and hopeful about the future . . . individually and together

---

If what God wants in our lives is for us to be at peace with the past, alive to the present, and hopeful about the future, then in what ways do you and your fellow council leaders need to set the past aside, give more attention to the present, and face your leadership team's particular fears with more hope?

3

Diversity, Change, Dissension

December 1990

In the fall of 1990, an article was published in the Reader's Digest that caused a stir inside the denomination. Under the title, "Look What They've Done to My Church," the author leveled the allegation that the Presbyterian Church was falling farther away from its roots. In several ways, it prompted the current ongoing engagement between evangelicals and progressives about the nature of the church. And it showed that we were becoming less and less able to speak the truth in love to one another.

One of the ongoing challenges we face in the church is how to understand our diversity. We are a diverse body as a denomination and as a presbytery. And likewise, most of our congregations reflect a good bit of diversity as well. The challenge we face in the church is similar to society's. We are part of an incredibly diverse culture and we struggle to find the right ways to celebrate our various cultural heritages and to minimize them for the sake of a common identity. We struggle with how much of our diversity is God's gift and how much it reflects human sin.

DIVERSITY, CHANGE, DISSENSION

The church has the opportunity to model for society the good ways to address diversity by remaining united without having to be unanimous in all things.

So, when articles such as a recent *Reader's Digest* piece appear ("Look What They Done to My Church," Fall 1990), our diversity in the church is put to the test. Make no mistake: it is an unkind article toward our church. It strikes the familiar theme of the distance between the pew and the national church. It sees only the negative. It encourages behaviors that undermine healthy dialogue within the family. And it invites defensiveness.

Thus far, our national leaders' response has included:

- sending three national mailings, including an eight-page blow-by-blow answer to the assertions made, sent to every pastor and clerk of session
- offering a list of the facts so we can answer the charges being made
- playing the "yes-but" game: "Yes," we say, "the critique may be partially true, but it doesn't tell the whole story." We counter with our stories of commissioning more missionaries than ever before (400 at the 1990 General Assembly). We mention our gifts of cartons of books to the Reformed seminaries in eastern Europe (the first books their libraries had received in forty years). Some see a half-empty glass while others see a glass half full.

Our diversity is God's gift, and our theology comes from a God who creates each of us with a unique configuration of gifts. It is a blessing if we welcome in it the opportunity to gain new understandings and a stronger faith. All this is true even if some of our diversity may reflect human sin.

General Assembly moderator ruling elder Price Gwyn has spent this year listening to our diverse church. In a recent meeting in Dallas, Texas, he reflected: "We're learning how to deal with our differences. It's tough. It's slow. There are no easy solutions. But I see hope. I see hope in that we've spelled out what kind of church we intend to be. We want to be a worshipping, witnessing, serving community of believers in Jesus Christ that is pluralistic, inclusive and diverse. We're not there yet, but people are beginning to catch the vision."

I think there are two clues to help us live better within God's diverse community. First, we do well to find ways to openly share our differences. That means being honest about our opinions, thoughts, and beliefs. It means being vulnerable enough to hear a different point of view or a dissenting opinion. And possibly be moved by it. The first clue is living with the notion that someone else's thoughts can be God's invitation to change our own. The second clue is to know "when to hold 'em and when to fold 'em," as Kenny Rogers sings in "The Gambler." There are appropriate moments to fully engage our differences and other right times to let them go for the sake of a common purpose.

Working together, as diverse as the church may be, is one of the great witnesses we make to the world. It takes openness, timing, hard work, prayer, wisdom, and a willingness to be led by God's Spirit and not our agendas. And every time we gather to discuss the great issues of life and faith, God gives us the opportunity to show the world how a diverse community of followers can know life and know it abundantly.

When has your council recently experienced a heated exchange over your community's diversity? What was the concern? In that moment, was the differences you experienced a reflection of God's doing or our failing? Why is it that some find it hard to consider the different views and perspectives of a brother/sister? How might your council respond rather than react to the next moment that comes your way?

4

The Shadow Side of the Sexuality Discussion

February 1992

Human sexuality is one of the most fundamental and complex parts of our identity. Those engaged in the religious journey look to God through the church for guidance and help. It was striking that the Presbyterian Church's 1991 Report on Human Sexuality was presented amidst the growing awareness of the crisis of sexual abuse, and for the church, clergy sexual abuse. Both continue to be significant challenges to the life of the church and in the world.

A recent news story noted that the General Assembly's (1991) response to the Task Force on Human Sexuality was selected as the year's number one religious news event. It was considered more significant than the release of the Dead Sea Scrolls, the conservative tightening of control over the Southern Baptist Convention, the United Church of Christ's support of active euthanasia, or the Orthodox Church's withdrawal from the National Council of Churches.

For all of the furor over the task force's report preceding the assembly and for all of the sighs of relief, the wept tears, or the numbed silence that followed the vote, there remains a stark realization: the conversation is not over.

Despite the hopes of some that the church would issue a clear declaration that would forever lay the matter to rest, the church chose to make a statement "for the time being." The comments of synod executive Rev. Bill Fogleman are noteworthy:

> Sexual, familiar, reproductive, relational and affectional arrangements are a major obsession of the human race at this time, and our recent engagement in Baltimore [site of the 1991 General Assembly] is but a ripple in a tidal wave of struggle to understand and to respond. . . . Everybody lost and everybody won in Baltimore, knowing full well that it was simply one more engagement in what will be a decade-long family struggle. And if you want to "get away from it," leaving the Presbyterian Church won't be enough! You'll need to vacate planet earth and cleanse your own psyche! And if you want the Church to stop talking about "it," so we can have just a little peace and quiet—this won't work either. God hasn't called us to escape, hide, or "go numb" in the head or the heart. Quite the contrary.

In spite of Bill's reminder that we cannot hide, a good part of me is ready for a little peace and quiet. Yet the news in the public square and the church continues to be filled with stories that reflect our inability to address our sexuality. It's not simply the headline stories of a Magic Johnson contracting the HIV virus or a Mike Tyson being convicted of rape. Last August a minister in a neighboring presbytery was charged with fourteen counts of sexual molestation of children. We agonize when any presbytery must confront the allegation that one of its ministers has betrayed a counseling relationship with sexual intimacy. The General Assembly legal staff report that they receive four to five calls a day seeking advice about charges of sexual misconduct. One to two new allegations are filed somewhere around our church every week.

The Shadow Side of the Sexuality Discussion

This is the shadow side of the sexuality discussion that the church cannot ignore. On the one hand, we are trying to define appropriate moral and ethical behavior, as with the report of the Human Sexuality Task Force. On the other hand, the church must address sexuality in terms of the consequences for inappropriate behavior. The larger church is learning what Eastern Oklahoma presbytery sadly learned years ago: you cannot ignore sexual misconduct.

So, thankfully, the General Assembly now has a sexual misconduct policy. Changes have been proposed to our Book of Discipline. National workshops are being offered to train response teams. We know that when an allegation of misconduct is made, the church must and will spend incredible amounts of energy, time and money.

But policy papers and response teams don't address the underlying truth that our sexuality is woven into the fabric of our very being. Sexuality is integral to our identity. And that is as true for ministers and church officers as it is for pew sitters.

The conversation ahead of us needs to continue—in both directions. Bill Fogleman is correct: God hasn't called us to escape, hide, or "go numb" in the head or the heart. Quite the contrary.

It is hard to talk about these matters before the moment when some new allegation surfaces. Is it better to wait until a crisis occurs? What's our message when we are silent? What's our message when we openly discuss human sexuality, even if clumsily addressed. And what might your council do to bring a more faithful engagement of this complex part of human life?

5

Searching for Ministers

June 1992

This reflection was shared in two presbyteries, first in 1992 and again in 1999. The 1999 report included the following data: In 1994, there were 1700 ministers in the Presbyterian Church (USA) seeking a new call, but only 950 congregations searching. Five years later, in 1999, the numbers reversed: there were 1300 ministers and 1600 congregations engaged in the search process. That's 24 percent fewer ministers and 68 percent more churches, compared to the 1994 numbers. 24 percent fewer ministers, 68 percent more churches.

―◇―

We spend an awful lot of time as a presbytery and as congregational leaders looking for the next minister to serve in our congregations. In recent years, the amount of time has increased because of certain trends, including: the trend toward unhealthy conflicts between pastors and congregations which leads to the trend toward shorter pastorates which leads to the trend toward longer search processes in the hopes of perfecting the selection and avoiding a short pastorate the next time. Those trends aren't likely to change soon. Committees on Ministry will work hard and experience the stress of the many demands placed upon them. Pastor nominating committees will work hard and face their versions of ecclesiastical stress. And congregations will wait, less and less patiently, for the answer to the question: Who will be our next minister?

Where we find the next minister is a question about the trees. The question in the forest is: Where will we find the next generation of ministers? To this question, a new report from the Task Force on Theological Education brings some light.

The report discusses the changing world of theological education and its impact on our students. In it, Dorothy Bass, associate professor at Valpraiso University, reflects on the changing environment:

> the secularization of the common school, the privatization and fragmentation of family life, the reported weakness of Christian education in the congregation, and the near demise of the religious publication, the student Christian movement and the recognizably denominational college have made it far more difficult for theological schools to do their job. Vast networks of spiritual formation, leadership recruitment, and preseminary academic preparation have dissipated. Those responsible for the theological education of clergy are now charged with accomplishing many tasks and dimensions of preparation that were once shared within a vital configuration.

Echoing her comment about the dissipation of a vast network of support and preparation were the comments I heard at a recent pastors' retreat. The minister spoke of how young people used to be encouraged to attend presbytery youth retreats, go to our regional conference centers, take leadership in our youth programs, be invited by a pastor or adult to consider the ministry, and if there were any inclination, be nurtured along the path to ordained ministry. The recruitment system was built on a strong Christian education program, an active mid-council youth ministry, and a recognition by most every church leader that he/she shares in the responsibility to enlist the next generation of ministers.

Where will we find the next generation of ministers? This is a question for all of us, not just other ministers or committees on preparation for ministry. One other comment from the report is noteworthy:

> A disturbing number of our students today are self-selected for ministry, rather than enlisted by the church for their skills and abilities in ministry. One of the most pernicious effects of the malaise of mainstream Protestantism is the reluctance and even refusal of the church to make the enlistment of ministers a high priority of the denomination as a whole.

This is no easy challenge. The call to ministry once brought with it the assurance of respect in the community and relatively low stress. Today it is the stress that is high and the esteem for the vocation that is low. Our society has de-valued such altruistic professions as teacher, social worker, and minister.

In concluding, the task force states in part:

> The problem of recruitment transcends the theological institutions and resists quick programmatic solutions. The church must ask if its future leadership should be chiefly self-selected. Despite the strong Reformed emphasis on the roles the whole church should play in evoking, testing and confirming the call to ministry, self-selection will become the norm unless church leaders and governing bodies take deliberate steps to reverse the trend. Persons of integrity, intelligence and spiritual depth must regularly be confronted, in the congregations, presbyteries, campus organizations and mission projects where they are already serving, with the possibility that they have a vocation to ministry. We challenge local congregations to make this confrontation one of their highest priorities.

When was the last time your congregation searched for a pastor? When was the last time your session endorsed a candidate for the ministry? What would you identify as important programs in your church that helped call a new generation of ministers? As you consider the future, what would be one helpful program or practice your council might do to identify, encourage and support a future generation?

6

Sea Changes for the Church

June 1993

In the early 1990s Loren Mead, founder of the Alban Institute, sensed a significant moment emerging in the church. His writing opened new doors for many of us in mid-council service and helped us see that the future church would be grounded in several new and important ideas.

Early last month, I spent a continuing education week with Loren Mead of the Alban Institute. Building on his book *The Once and Future Church*, our conversation focused on the impact these changes have on a mid-council of the church, such as our presbytery. Here are some recurring thoughts about where we seem to be headed.

1. The age of Christendom is over. No longer is the edge of the mission frontier in some far off place; it is on the doorstep of every congregation. The primary ministers in the new frontier will be the members of our congregations.

2. The era of rapid church growth in the twentieth century followed the Second World War. The hallmarks of this season

included many new church developments, the growth of the church school, the ecumenical movement, camp and conference programs, a high response to men's and women's groups, and youth ministries. Christians today have been imprinted by this age. In essence, Mead says, "We have misfiled the past under the present." We are trying to re-create the past and it will not work.

3. One imprint from the past is that first-class churches have a full-time pastor serving them. Congregations that can't afford a pastor have been subconsciously labeled second class. Mead challenges this imprint, suggesting that our small churches today are wrestling with a reality that more and more congregations will face in the coming years: how to be in ministry without full-time pastoral leadership. The small congregations today are pioneering what many of the rest of us will face in the future.

4. One special challenge will be to help all of our congregations become financially independent. We must reconsider whether our patterns of financial grant giving have created dependence, or have helped them grow to independence. We must do this in a time when there will be more and more financial burdens facing the congregation including: increasing medical insurance, possible taxation of church property, governmental limits on charitable giving, housing allowances for ministers, and the increasing costs of litigation and liability insurance.

During our week, Mead went on to identify five ways presbyteries and other mid-councils can help their congregations:

a. *Help churches when they get into trouble.* Financial crunches, conflicts between liberals and conservatives, and misconduct issues will continue to be present in coming years. The presbytery needs to have intervention plans in place (conflict management teams, emergency financial aid, etc.).

b. *Motivate churches.* Inertia may be one of the great enemies that congregations will have in the coming years. It will be easier to keep doing the same old thing (even when it doesn't work). At times, the presbytery must be ready to help jump start congregations in new directions.

c. *Help churches grieve.* Congregations face loss all the time—loss of pastors and particular leaders, loss of buildings, loss of an old vision that is no longer realistic. This loss also includes the recognition that the old ways of being the church aren't working. As an existing congregation makes new changes, a new church is being formed, and an old church is being set aside, all accompanied by an appropriate sense of pain, loss, and sorrow. Can a presbytery help its congregations say goodbye?

d. *Affirm churches.* The presbytery must build bridges with its congregations and among them. We need to affirm the successful ministries that our congregations are doing, and avoid suggesting that every church has to do the same set of ministries all in the same way. Most of all, we need to declare that the ministry of the local congregation is the ministry of the Presbyterian Church (USA).

e. *Offer technical assistance.* Congregations will continue to need specialized help (raising money, conducting mission studies, searching for pastors, etc.) that only the presbytery can provide. We need to have strategies to consult with congregations about their individual needs.

All of this suggests that if a mid-council's vision is to support its congregation, it will do well to consider offering fewer programs and more consultation services with its congregations. It will do well to face its own financial realities and pay for the programs it does offer more with participant fees and less through its operating budget. It will need to send its leaders more into congregational engagement and less into committee meetings. And it will need to simplify its organization to make it more flexible and responsive to new concerns and needs. Much to think about as we consider tomorrow.

As a council, where do you go to discover new insights? To the leaders/officers? To the staff? To wise individuals in the body? What can you do to discipline your life so that time is regularly given to this discovery? Reflect on one key insight that has come to your council in the last twelve months, and what you have done to evaluate it and to make it important to your council's life.

7

Doing Theology

September 1993

This reflection was prompted by the departure of the Rev. Dr. David Buttrick from the PC(USA). David was one of my professors at Pittsburgh Theological Seminary, who talked the talk and walked the walk. His theological posture and integrity left him no choice but to say goodbye.

David Buttrick is an important person to me. Twenty years ago he was my professor of preaching at Pittsburgh Seminary. While I was never a star pupil, I appreciated and loved this man. He is a man of integrity. In the mid-1970s he left the seminary when, during a financial crisis the seminary board laid off several members of the support staff, the cooks and custodians, while giving salary increases to the faculty. It was an offense to David's understanding of the Christian community, and the seminary lost one of its finest professors. Over this past summer, David wrote an article about his leaving the Presbyterian Church to join the United Church of Christ.

In the article, David writes that once we were a great people. He talks about the great days when the Presbyterian Church stood up to Joe McCarthy, stood with civil rights leaders, and stood for church union. He fondly remembers that we "Presbyterians scrapped over theological issues and, what's more, scrapped in public." Then we became a frightened people. We left the inner cities and put our money in the suburbs. We became a more cautious denomination, after contributing to the Angela Davis defense fund and after the reunion of 1983. We are desperately concerned to hold on to ourselves in a time of cultural change, even though our Lord sternly warned against those who would "preserve their life." . . . We have become so safe we may yet bore each other to death.

David's key critique concerns the Scriptures.

> So what has troubled me? Is it the triumph of Karl Barth? Yes, partially. In the sixties, I read through the many volumes of Barth's *Church Dogmatics* and, for a decade, was swept by the supposed staunchness of "biblical theology." But, though we Presbyterians cheer Barth's Barmen bravery, we forget that, later, he retired from social courage into a kind of defensive biblicism, as has our Presbyterian Church. Presbyterians now clutch the Bible as if, convictionally, it were a fourth part of the Trinity. As a result in Presbyterian circles, there are enlarging tensions between preaching the Gospel and preaching the Bible, between thinking theologically and merely doing "biblical study." We seem to be using the slogan *sola scriptura* as an excuse to avoid the real task of our own theological revision.

I find David's departing words haunting because they make me wonder if my vision of the church's renewal is so focused on the Scriptures that I have forgotten it is only a first step. Like many of you, I have stood up and denounced the impoverished biblical knowledge in the Presbyterian Church and that too few people know the Bible and read it regularly. But David's words remind me that there is something beyond a knowledge of Scripture that God expects from each one of us: *the work of our own theological revision.*

One of the simplest ways to understand theology is to remember Jesus's question to Peter, "Who do you say that I am?"

Jesus didn't ask, "What do the Scriptures say about the Christ?" Jesus' question is personal, and every disciple must answer it. Peter's answer, "You are the Christ" reflected his theological revision. And it is not enough to simply repeat Peter's words. We must do our own wrestling to reach this conviction, even if it means undertaking many revisions in our thinking and understanding along the way. The purpose of theological discussion is not consensus or unanimity, but each participant's articulation of the faith. It is our theology that contains answers to the important questions about God and humanity and the way God creates, renews, and redeems life. And our answers influence how we respond to life's changing circumstances, how we interpret what happens around us and inside us.

Doing theology means reflecting on what happens to us and asking what we're learning about God and ourselves and the things that truly matter. No other person can do this theological work for us, not the pastor or even the preacher. It is personal work, but it is not private work. We Presbyterians do this in community, in conversation with forebears and fellow travelers. We allow the words of those who have gone before us and those who journey with us to shape the words we use to declare what we believe.

So, place David Buttrick's comments about theological revision alongside the life of our presbytery. When was the last time we had a robust theological debate on the floor of one of our meetings? When was the last time someone stood up and said, "I see God at work in this decision we are about to make"? When was the last time the discussion at mealtime drew out your personal convictions about life and faith? I'm convinced all of us have been doing our theological work over these last several years, but we've not shared that work with one another enough. And I suspect we haven't encouraged this activity in the life of the disciples entrusted to our congregations' care.

I regret David's decision to part our company. He leaves a haunting question that, if left unaddressed, will unravel the fabric of our life together. In this community, do we know our theological convictions and do we live with the courage of those convictions?

Doing Theology

What are some core theological convictions that guide your decisions and commitments as a council? In what ways are those convictions translated into your council's behaviors and actions? Reflect on a moment (past or present) where holding a particular conviction pressed or is pressing into your current life. What will be required of you to hold onto that conviction?

8

Anxiety, Leadership and Re-Imagining

March 1994

In late 1993, a controversial ecumenical conference was held in which national Presbyterian staff were involved in the planning and in which many Presbyterians attended. The progressive ideas shared at this event became very controversial. The reports by conservative church groups led to a firestorm. The church eventually worked its way through the crisis at the next General Assembly meeting, held in Wichita, Kansas. I suspect however, that "Re-Imagining" has taken a place next to "Angela Davis" as among the great troubles in the PCUSA over the last fifty years.

About a month ago, Marney attended a worship conference in Dallas for three days and two nights, and while she was away, I was solo parent to our three children. They're now fifteen, twelve, and six. Marney periodically makes such trips which become traumatic events for me. I can't quite figure out how to be an executive and a single parent without losing more hair than I can afford to lose. Each time she leaves we make lists, stock food, listen to her advice, think we're ready, and then after she leaves, life falls apart.

Last month, the collapse happened on the second day, during a two-hour dinner break sandwiched between two very difficult church meetings for me. Within seconds of walking in the door, all three kids had asked for help. My six-year-old proudly said, "I have homework Dad, can you help me?" My twelve-year-old had a special project. And my fifteen-year-old was stewing about a science report that involved visiting the zoo and researching animals.

The fifteen-year-old needed help printing the title page of a report for which he had yet to start his research, let alone write, and would have been quite happy to call it quits with that. When I suggested he might use the new computer encyclopedia to do a little research, I found myself giving an emergency refresher course to a reluctant student.

My twelve-year-old then told me he'd volunteered to make a replica model of Shakespeare's Globe Theatre with balsa wood. He was ready to start cutting pieces, having already retrieved Marney's exacto knife . . . except that he needed help calculating the circumference of a circle that could then be divided into twenty-four sections.

I was working on this geometry when my six-year-old thrust her homework assignment in front of me. With a face reflecting a mixture of pride (I have some homework, Dad) and panic (oh no, I have some homework, help me!), she read, "Name the famous groundhog and where he comes from." I think, "Great, this'll be easy." We bumped my oldest from the computer to look for an answer that wasn't in there! Oh, Groundhog Day was explained in a one-sentence article, but neither the little fella's name nor his place of residence were mentioned. And by this time, I was starting to panic. I was desperate enough to call two friends, moderators of sessions mind you, and ask "Do you know the name of the famous groundhog?"

All of this was compounded by my decision to not eat tuna casserole for the second night in a row. At my oldest child's suggestion, I ordered a pizza from a Little Caesar's three miles away. By the time I finally returned home and we sat down to a dinner of lukewarm pizza, my oldest son Matt, said with a straight face, "You don't do well when Mom's gone, do you Dad."

I share all this with you because it strikes me that Matt's question has something to say about the church right now. We are an anxious denomination. We have experienced three national controversies at our General Assembly meetings over the last four years: the human sexuality report, the homosexuality discussion and most recently, the Re-Imagining ecumenical women's conference last fall. All of this has been on top of a major reduction in the number of national staff we employ, and a subsequent structural reorganization. The statistical fuel that fans our anxious flames is the decline—in members and dollars and trust. And what's frustrating as hell is that despite whatever good work may be happening in the name of Jesus Christ, it is overshadowed by the anxiety and confusion we experience with each new controversy.

For the last three months, the Re-Imagining Conference has brought out the worst in us. Brothers and sisters in the faith have attacked and parried, and accused others of irresponsibility. They have framed and reframed the issues in inflammatory and emotional language. Admittedly the issues are complex and numerous: theological orthodoxy, freedom of thought, speech and expression, faithful stewardship, accountability in a connectional church, identity and integrity in an ecumenical setting, among them. The General Assembly Council has now spent untold hours in anxious discussion and its subsequent decisions are likely to be unsatisfactory to both critic and defender.

The irony, of course, is that this latest controversy is not as important as some would think; but neither is it as trivial a matter as others would have us believe. For whatever that was right or wrong about this conference, you and I can analyze speeches on tapes and second guess motives and still miss the opportunity to face our real fear. We're afraid to talk with each other. I think both liberals and conservatives are happier talking about the "other" than engaging in an honest, respectful conversation that helps us understand each other's faith story and journey with God. I think we've become an institution that doesn't want to admit how theologically fuzzy it really is. And, as the leaders of this institution, I don't think we know what to do about the deep diversity found within our body. We hold truly differing views of Scripture and theological authority, of the redeeming work of Jesus Christ and the good news that we are to proclaim. We differ in how we see this world, its people and its resources. I think we're afraid to share our beliefs and our doubts because we don't want to name any boundaries that may fence us in, or out.

"You don't do well when Mom's gone, do you Dad?" The bigger question I hear behind my son's observation is this: can we tell what's missing when we see our church so anxious and fearful? Part of the answer is very simple. We have lost our ability to be a people of honest dialogue and theological discourse at all levels of the church. And we must recover this.

I wonder what would happen if the Presbyterian Church (USA) took all the energy and money and time we are currently putting into more rules and changes to the Book of Order for one year and instead, underwrite an honest conversation about our confessions and beliefs. I wonder how different this presbytery would be if we committed an hour at every meeting to theological discourse among ourselves, without some issue to vote upon. Or, if the leaders in the presbytery—all of us—agreed to take turns sharing our personal stories of the faith as a regular part of our presbytery meetings, committee meetings and retreats. I wonder what would happen if each session meeting included some elder sharing his or her personal statement of faith?

So often in a controversy, it's tempting to look to others for leadership, which is precisely what we cannot afford to do. That's not to suggest that we can't expect responsible and accountable leadership from others. But each one of us is a leader in this church. We are the ones who must stay focused on the truly important things: our trust in God, the redeeming and hopeful love we know in Jesus Christ, the bonds of fellowship within the body, our interdependence and mutual accountability. We must stay focused and committed to the ongoing work of journeying together as a reformed and always being reformed people.

If we want a more faithful and less anxious church, it doesn't begin in Louisville but rather right here in Tulsa, with you and me.

Sometimes the leadership experience isolates us, especially when others lay their expectations at our feet. Expectations for a quick solution. Expectations for a solution that pleases everyone. Remember a time when you experienced the isolation and tension. What did you do to remind the entire body that everyone is important and has responsibility for solutions, not simply pointing out problems?

9
Naming the Challenges

June 1994

As the conflict surrounding the Re-Imagining Conference continued, I found myself listening to many voices all seeking to reduce the source of the conflict to a particular issue. Like a plate of spaghetti, no one strand defines the entire plate, just as no one issue defines the dilemma before us.

The controversy surrounding the Re-Imagining Conference continues. By now, thousands of letters have been sent to the General Assembly offices and the General Assembly Council. Forty-eight overtures have been forwarded to this year's General Assembly meeting. Two-hundred sixty-nine sessions have taken action to withdraw, or temporarily escrow, financial support. There's more going on than simply the complaints about a four-day conference.

We are a troubled denomination with a divided constituency and increasingly unsure about the future. More often than not, what holds us together (unity) receives quiet and modest acknowledgement while the things that pull us apart (diversity) gathers up all of our emotional and passionate energy. Many are being weighed down by fear and are lashing out in frustration.

As we explore the deeper issues, we do well to remember that this is not the first time the Presbyterian Church has known controversy. From its earliest beginnings, American Presbyterians have engaged in disagreements about fundamentals of the faith and the focus of our mission (think Old School / New School, the Auburn Declaration, Civil Rights, the Ordination of Women). And before that, the Reformation itself was a massive, controversial re-framing of the Catholic Church at the time. It's quite possible that the hurt and pain of this current controversy is God's latest invitation to refocus the church and stretch its people. If we are not open to rethinking what we understand, reaffirming what we deeply believe, reimagining what we envision, and reclaiming what we hold dear, then how on God's good earth can we say we are people Reformed and always being reformed?

So, our context is important. We are wise to remember that:

- we live in a time when national institutions, including religious denominations, are increasingly unpopular and national leaders are subsequently mistrusted
- we live in a time when it's too tempting to focus on our weaknesses rather than our strengths
- we live in a time when too many people think more data is needed to solve our problems, when we value empathy rather than responsible behavior, and when we fear that strong leaders will become autocrats.

In a recent letter to the Church, Jim Andrews, the stated clerk of our General Assembly writes:

> It is my view that the Re-Imagining Conference is not the cause of the current furor in our church, but only an occasion for releasing a huge reservoir of discontent, even anger . . . Presbyterians stand on the brink of serious damage to the very fabric of our part of the body of Christ . . . the various regions of our church and the governing bodies may no longer work as closely together in carrying out mission, nor feel as great a sense of partnership. [Among the things we must address are] the loss of

spiritual vitality, the need for full financial disclosure, the recovery of trust, our failure to communicate, the need for flexibility and innovation, and the absence of civility and the decline of rational debate.

As I reflect on what I hear from you, a picture of the deeper issues before us is coming into focus:

1. Can we be a family of faith where relationships are as important as principles? Will we do less talking *about* each other and start committing more time to honest, respectful conversations that help us understand the other person's faith story and journey with God?

2. Do we want to be a church that insists on uniformity of belief and practice? If not, how much diversity of belief/practice will/can/should we tolerate?

3. Can we reaffirm a way to be one church when we disagree about the deity, life and work of Christ, and authority of Scripture? For some, faithfulness means learning to interpret the Bible through the lens of personal experiences and perspectives, while for others, faithfulness means interpreting our personal experiences through the Bible.

4. Will we restore respect and civility to our disagreements? Until conservatives criticize other conservatives for their outlandish behaviors, and liberals criticize other liberals for theirs, our conflicts are likely to remain ugly. Frankly, it is more than a matter of civility; it is a reflection of an attitude arising out of Scripture. Scriptural Christians, living as the Body of Christ with its many parts, simply don't treat each other with the disrespect that has been shown in some quarters.

5. Will we continue to add more rules and regulations to cover up the lack of depth in our relationships?

6. Will we let the passions of a few, some liberal and others conservative, the ones who are the most conflicted and who voice their concerns in emotional and inflammatory language play

tug of war with the church's energy and resources, intelligence, imagination and love?

7. In what ways will we affirm our unity/diversity? Can our Book of Confessions help us claim a common enough faith? Can our Book of Order sustain a common commitment to work together? Can we welcome the diversity of gifts, opinions, views (male/female; rich/poor; racial/ethnic) that comprise God's good creation?

8. Can we build a consensus anymore? Or are our loyalties to a particular interest group and its narrower perspective stronger than our loyalty to the whole body?

9. Can we affirm the need for a denomination, when the initiatives for mission are increasingly framed at the local level? What do we want our "national" church leaders to do, both volunteers and staff? What will we do to rebuild trust with our national leaders?

As the current controversy has both theological and ecclesiastical elements, so do these deeper issues. Some of what we need to engage reflects our beliefs about God, Christ, and the Holy Spirit. Some of what we need to discuss is ecclesiastical in nature and how we make decisions, spend our money, and who does what on behalf of whom.

Like it or not, last November's conference has prompted a significant moment for the Presbyterian and Reformed community. Engaging these deeper issues with our full attention, our prayerful reflection, our open minds, and our respectful engagement just might lead us into a transforming experience for the good of God's kingdom.

The ancient wisdom is true: out of crisis comes opportunity. A church building burns down and new directions in mission are created with a new building. A long pastorate ends and the people share more responsibility and ownership of the congregation's life. Funding support for a church council dramatically declines and a simpler vision relying less on staff and more on the people emerges. As a council, name a current challenge you face and identify some positive outcomes that could emerge.

10

Leading Change with Explorers and Benefactors

September 1994

During the course of a life journey, all of us are introduced to significant ideas that shape and sustain us. In the midst of the denominational controversies that dominated my attention in the early 1990s, the ideas about "family systems" became very important. Some of those ideas were first introduced in a lecture Rabbi Edwin Friedman gave to then Texas governor Ann Richards and her staff, entitled "The Challenge of Change and the Spirit of Adventure." His insights pushed me away from the anxiety and toward encouraging a hopeful approach to change.

There's a saying that I know you all have heard: If it isn't broken, don't fix it. Recently I discovered a counterpoint bit of advice: If it's not working, quit doing the same thing.

Periodically we have reflected on the world of change in the church with the help of outside leaders and inside conversations. We even have a special work group devoted simply to raising important questions about the paradigm shifts we are experiencing.

The times have changed and so have many of our people. Now they are more interested in personal security than in institutional loyalty. Many of our neighbors are basically consumers and not givers. They treat the church like the marketplace. The church's mission is no longer over there, but right here on our doorsteps. The issues are all too familiar.

And I think our conversations are beginning to make a difference. Ask any group of mainline Protestants about the state of the church, and you are likely to hear the story of declining membership, decreasing commitment and increasing concern about institutional survival. Then ask that same group of people what they intend to do about it and the answer will likely be, "We need to do more of what we used to do." Alban Institute founder, Loren Mead, says, "Too many of us have misfiled the past under the future."

There's a sense in which we have gotten ourselves stuck.

Understandably so. When the pressure is on to turn things around quickly, we tend to look hardest at making minor adjustments to old ways that were once successful, and we tend to lock our imaginations onto solutions from the past. Rabbi Edwin Friedman calls this imaginative gridlock. Several years ago, Friedman wrote a paper on the occasion of the five hundredth anniversary of the European arrival to the Americas by Christopher Columbus. He entitled the paper "The Challenge of Change and the Spirit of Adventure."

In the article Friedman quotes the Nuremberg Chronicles of 1492 which described the European household as depressed. Europe was in the wake of the plagues, the breakdown of the Feudal order, the problems within the church and the economic reality that the Moors had encircled and cut Europe off from the markets in the East. Europe was, to Friedman, a depressed extended family, stuck in imaginative gridlock.

He goes on to note three key signs of this kind of gridlock:

1. people keep trying the same old ways with more and more energy, using more and more resources, and the lack of significant results makes them try harder

2. everyone keeps trying to solve old questions with new answers rather than changing the questions being asked
3. a polarization develops between extremes so that no one can imagine the infinite range of other possibilities in between.

With this in mind, it's not too hard to see the imaginative gridlock in our churches. For example:

- We have become too focused on Sunday morning to grow the church. Inviting friends to our worship service is too limiting. Sunday morning isn't the only time we can worship our God and it is not the only time some could or would choose to worship. Worship is central to our faith, but it may be that growing the future church will ask us to offer more than one time each week for people to gather in worship and praise.

- We are stuck in our mission imagination. We keep funding the same mission projects year after year: *this* hunger program or *that* care center. With the mission frontier on our doorstep, we do well to reopen our imaginations to how we might serve the needs of God's people

- We are stuck in how we teach the faith, relying too much on the church school classroom. Too many of today's parents and grandparents are not prepared to tell their children the story of God's good news in Christ. So, home conversations seldom if ever include a discussion of the faith.

When we keep trying old solutions that don't work and in frustration, return to them again and again with more and more of our resources... and when we keep trying to answer old questions instead of asking new ones... and when our vision is reduced to "either-or" thinking and we're cut off from exploring the possibilities in between, we've become stuck.

In his article Friedman finally asks, "Are we to believe that Europe simply changed its mind?" Of course not. Europe eventually moved out of its corporate depression to discover a new world with all its possibilities. What did it take to do this? Among other things, it took the bold leadership of some who were willing to explore new possibilities, such as the leadership of Bartholomew Diaz who rounded the Cape of Good Hope at the tip of Africa in 1488. It took people like Diaz and Columbus and Verrazano and Magellan. It took the leadership of the explorer. But, Friedman notes, it also took the generosity of the benefactor: of people like Queen Isabella who funded Columbus. It took people like Prince Henry the Navigator who, seventy years before Columbus, funded repeated trips down the coast of Africa to see how far one could venture south.

The message from Friedman is that the church needs both explorers and benefactors—pioneers and patrons—if we are to move imaginatively toward the future. In most big businesses today, we would call this research and development.

Where are our dreamers and risk-takers? Where are the ones who have an idea percolating and need a little encouragement to try something new? And, where are the people who see the need for setting aside some of our resources to explore new possibilities? Whether it is personal gift giving or advocating that our budgets include some grant giving, it is time for us to fund new exploration. Given our stuckness, this is a great time for the explorers and benefactors among us to step forward.

———◇———

In your council and community, it is likely that some people will be the explorers and others the benefactors. And those folks will change with different opportunities. Discuss an opportunity currently before your council. Share the ways you might identify the folks who could help you go exploring.

11

The Church of Christ Uniting

June 1995

One major change to the church in the last thirty years has been the diminishing witness of the ecumenical movement. United by God's call to change the world, it was denominations working ecumenically that paved the way of much of the church's social witness. Today ecumenism is celebrated less and less on the national stage and expressed more and more by congregations working locally. Nearly gone are the efforts to articulate and live together as the one Body of Jesus Christ. That is what made COCU (Church of Christ Uniting) so exciting.

———◊———

We all know that there once was a time when a family of Presbyterians moving in to a new city would only consider another Presbyterian congregation for their new church home. Today, Lutherans, Disciples, Episcopalians, Methodists—our people are choosing a church home on the basis of congregational and not denominational identity. People are choosing a church because: (a) they like the preacher, or (b) they like the program . . . and they care very little about the differences in understandings of the sacraments, and even less about whether the congregation is governed by a vestry, a board, or a session. This melting pot reality to today's congregational life creates problems in membership education and officer recruitment. It's not been good news to staunch denominational loyalists, who cringe when a new member, coming from anything but a Presbyterian identity, is quickly elected to be an elder.

As some folks continue to wrestle with denominational issues of mission, identity and our divisions, there have been others wrestling with the brokenness that exists within the larger body of Christ. These folks recognize that the reconciliation of the whole Christian community is an important part of God's reconciling work in the world.

The ecumenical movement has taken many forms through the years—councils of churches, consolidation of congregations, mergers of denominations—among them. At next month's General Assembly, we Presbyterians are going to consider a new ecumenical proposal that would establish a covenant among nine denominations. The covenant is called the Church of Christ Uniting. Nine denominations are being asked to become part of something bigger than just a denomination. We would continue to be a Presbyterian Church, and also make a witness to the larger reality of Christ's one body.

In particular, the nine denominations would recognize each other's members, celebrate the Lord's supper together, recognize the ordination of each other's ministers, work together in mission, and form something called covenanting councils.

In all honesty, the COCU proposal is making many of us nervous. How on God's good earth could Presbyterians and Methodists be reconciled when we understand the word "bishop" in such different ways? How could we ever establish a new congregation together? The answer may be that God is doing the creating anyway by creating today's melting pot congregations. Besides, look at how the religious community banded together in response to the Oklahoma City bombing two months ago. We moved toward each other, worshipped together, raised funds for a common relief effort, and set up an interfaith group to oversee the ongoing work. Or, consider that recently there was a communion service for blacks and whites in north Tulsa to come together, something that would have been unheard of not so long ago.

The Church of Christ Uniting. I like this phrase because it reminds me that even if we had a perfect Presbyterian church, whatever that might be, we would still be incomplete. God would not be happy with our perfection because we would still face the challenge of reconciling the whole body of Jesus Christ.

The Church of Christ Uniting. This is a compelling vision, even if it ends up not to be a vision for this time and place. Twenty years ago, a vision found its time and place among us: a church divided by the Civil War gathered itself into one new body in 1983, the Presbyterian Church (USA). Surely that reunion won't be our last.

How would you characterize your congregation/council in terms of its unity in belief and witness? What does the phrase "one in Christ" mean? What might your council do to make that oneness visible to other communions and with other communions to the world?

12

Leadership and the Generations

September 1995

In my experience being the subject of the annual performance review was a mixed blessing. Some were helpful. Others were atrocious. One in particular prompted a good bit of reflection around the question, "What am I saying by the way I lead?"

Over the summer, I had several conversations with some friends, both inside and outside the presbytery. The conversations were focused on the issue of leadership in the church, and in particular, my leadership as an executive presbyter. I've appreciated the gentleness of your humor about my energy level, the latest version of which comes from Charlie Freeland who said that pastors greet one another now asking, "and what were you doing with your spare time before Wasserman arrived?" I've been grateful too, for the positive and negative comments several of you have offered about my leadership style. These conversations have been the occasion for me to ask two questions: "What does the church need from the leadership of an executive presbyter?" And, "What am I saying about leadership by the way I lead?" There is both a personal and an intellectual element to my answers.

To begin, permit me to offer four personal stories.

- I grew up in the 1950s and both my parents had careers outside the home. My father worked for an insurance company and my mother was a violinist in the Cincinnati Symphony Orchestra. Because of Mom's rehearsals and concerts, I remember my father cooking our meals on many nights. I look back and realize now that they were demonstrating a model of shared leadership that would not only affect my home life, but my professional one as well.

- The first minister who engaged me in a serious conversation about ministry was the Methodist pastor of my high school and college years. He said that, in many ways, his goal was to put himself out of a job. I remember thinking that an odd thing to say. But now I understand that he was trying to lead by empowering others to claim their calling as servants of Jesus Christ.

- I went to college and seminary in the late 1960s and early 1970s. Those were disruptive times, and I had my first adult leadership experience with a student organization called the National Union of Theological Students (NUTS, for short). I remember that in January 1972, we successfully found funding and organized a national gathering of seminary students to talk about the concerns of war and peace. And I learned that effective leadership can make good things happen.

- When Marney and I graduated from seminary, we had a vision: to share our calls somewhere in the church. Our initial exploration was a most unhappy experience. One congregation in Detroit invited us to interview and then tried to talk us out of the idea of working together in ministry. They even brought in the presbytery's leadership to denounce the idea of a clergy couple sharing one ministry. We kept up the search until we found a congregation in Iowa that didn't ask the question "why?" but responded with "why not?" And I learned that leadership is grounded in vision/calling/purpose and must be persistent, even sometimes to the point of stubbornness.

Leadership and the Generations

My doctor of ministry thesis was on leadership in the church. I share this because I'm aware of how things out of your past can come back to haunt you. Even old school papers. When I reread my dissertation recently, I experienced a pinch or two as I reviewed what I wrote.

1. Leadership in a democratic society is more a matter of having the authority to influence than it is having the power to decide.
2. Leadership is only possible where there is trust in the group. Where trust is broken, there can be no leading.
3. Leadership skills can be taught, or as someone once said, "Good leaders are good learners."
4. Leadership needs to display three qualities: (a) a caring and respectful attitude, (b) a participatory approach to putting decisions into action, and (c) a flexibility about people and structures.

Both the stories from my past and the ideas from my studies remain important to me as I think about what I bring to the work of leadership. Added to this has been a new thought: leadership expectations are a generational matter. That is, different generations have different expectations and attitudes toward their leaders. It's not so much a matter of growing into a more mature attitude about leadership, but rather that my generation has a different expectation than yours and that's something we will carry with us throughout all our years.

Someone recently reminded me that there are primarily four generations of Americans currrently living. They are the "GI" generation, the silent generation, the boomers and the 13ers. A friend recently wrote in a letter to me:

> We may need to learn to see generational differences as we see dialects in language, prone to some misunderstanding and needing steady clarification. For example, older generations are more covert and cautious about control. You Boomers are very up front about the need to

control, and very forthcoming and specific about desired outcomes. That is why when Boomers delegate to Silent and GI generational folks, there are nearly always some misunderstandings.

The primary question for all of us: *What are we saying by the way we lead?* What am I trying to convey through my leadership as an executive presbyter? Or you, as a pastor or elder? In thinking about this, four ideas come to mind:

a. what's important is the centrality of faith and the vision that accompanies it—the executive presbyter needs to challenge the presbytery's thinking and motivate the presbytery to action

b. what's important to me is the need to balance concern for getting the job done with a concern for the people affected by the work

c. what's important is the posture of the servant—exercising authority by providing the necessary information, reflections and opinions that assist those with the responsibility to make decisions

d. what's important is to foster a leadership style that nurtures mutual support, demonstrates the importance of staying connected, is visible, and demonstrates an ability to hear criticism and be ready to learn from one's mistakes

We all want to serve well. And it does us good to occasionally step back and reflect on our leadership style: what are we saying by the way we lead?

We all want to lead well. Make a list of three to four important ideas about your personal leadership. Share those with the others on your council's leadership team. Look for the common themes and build a statement together of some key ideas for your team.

13

Doing Better with Our Disagreements

March 1996

Disagreements are messy experiences because, when they first surface, it is unclear as to whether they will be helpful, as in clarifying and building up relationships, or unhelpful, as in complicating and tearing them down. Church conflicts are uncomfortable because we forget how to focus on issues while loving the people. While it's true that the church has always known conflict, it's also true that we tend to perceive our conflicts as the worst ever!

Several years ago one of our ministers told me the story of a church fight that happened between two of the members. The little church building had been destroyed by a tornado and the congregation decided to rebuild at a different location a couple of blocks away. To honor the past, one member, an amateur artist, painted a picture of the former building and hung it on a wall in the new narthex. An older woman, a longtime pillar and troublemaker was upset that the big walnut tree wasn't in the painting. She told him to take it down and paint it in, and he refused. After a few such exchanges, the woman took decisive action. Being something of an amateur artist herself, she took the picture home and proceeded to paint in the disputed tree. When she brought it back to church, the original artist was more than upset, partly because it wasn't a very good tree. So, he took it home and scratched out his signature. He rehung it and the pastor showed me where it hangs to this day, tree and erased signature, and nobody dares touch it!

Gentle humor aside, the concern I want to raise with you is that we are experiencing an increasing number of disputes in our churches. Six new conflicts over the last three months in the churches in our presbytery. Pastors are at the center of some of them. Their performances are being challenged, or their integrity questioned. In others, elders are caught in power struggles between the older and younger generations. There have been dramatic resignations. There have been not so subtle threats to withhold pledges and support. There have been angry outbursts, including some swearing. There have been lengthy letters accusing, defending, blaming others, playing victim. Thankfully, none of these have turned into a Saturday night saloon brawl just yet.

I suppose it's old news that we Presbyterians don't do well with our disagreements. We can usually count on one ugly fight developing at each General Assembly meeting, and this coming meeting in July promises to be no exception. What's of greater concern is the inability of our congregational leaders to guide our churches through its conflicts. We're not doing well and we're not doing anything about it. We're not insisting there be a modicum of civility among those engaged in a conflict. We're not holding people accountable for their inappropriate anger, for their disruptive behaviors or their indirect attacks, where the whisper of a rumor can cast a shadow of doubt about someone's competence or integrity.

Why are our people fighting so much? Is it frustration that what we seek to be as the church isn't happening quickly enough? Is it anger from the grief that the church of forty years ago is not the church today? It's instructive to listen to people explain the church fights they observe. In an ecumenical gathering last month with the area Lutheran, Methodist, and Episcopal bishops, I was struck by our common plight and some of their insights. People don't have much loyalty these days, they said . . . not only to the denomination, but also to their congregation. When people join the church, they don't bring a commitment to stay together when disagreements surface. There is no commitment to learn to live with each other. And, too many assume that membership in the church means ownership, instead of trusteeship and stewardship.

Perhaps more troublesome is how the culture has taught the church to settle its conflicts. The culture teaches that it is acceptable to engage an adversary in uncivil ways. That it is acceptable to explode in anger. That it's acceptable to tell them to "go to hell." That it's acceptable to push and push and push until we get our way, to create winners and losers, to insist on our rights without regard for the common good, to triangulate and avoid the person we're upset with and to attack and then, when challenged, to defend ourselves by playing the victim and blaming others for our actions.

Well, you and I know that these behaviors are not acceptable. We may disagree and in fact, we will disagree because, thank God, we're not all the same. We will disagree and when we do, God expects us to treat each other with respect, honesty, care and love, and the only thing I know to do is to tell you that we all have some work to do. We have work to do in how we deal with our own anger and our own grieving, in how we help others in our congregations speak the truth in love so that our disagreements don't become bar room brawls.

Perhaps it is time to take some preventative action, including some focused reading, leadership training, and honest conversation. Persistent fighting, whether in a denomination or a congregation, is ultimately the way of death because it drains our energy and resources away from Christ's mission, from our worship and our witness to the world. It's time we realize that helping each other work through our conflicts, staying together in a community that will not be broken when disagreements break out and living in congregations that will hold us accountable when we stray from the civil and Christ-like path are all a part of Christ's mission, too.

Listen More, Laugh Often, Love Always

Recall a time when your council was involved in a sustained conflict. Tell the story together, including the ways you tried to address the issues. Remembering that in God's economy, our differences will continue to lead to disagreement but not necessarily conflicts, create a list of values that you want to guide your leadership team as you address future disagreements.

14

Being Clear

June 1996

The 1990s were stressful in the church for many reasons, among them: a growing awareness of the sea change related to the end of Christendom, and the persistent anxiety about embattled national church conflicts. Many leaders found themselves articulating those basic foundations to which they hoped all could agree. Here's mine:

I came across a newsletter article from a Lutheran church the other day from *Eculaugh* (*Eculaugh* was a subscription email newsletter in the 1990s containing humorous church-related anecdotes). It was entitled "You Just May Want to Study the Bible":

- If you think Psoriasis is a book in the Old Testament . . .
- If you think an epistle is the wife of an apostle . . .
- If you think Colossians are something you wear on your feet in the rain . . .
- If you think bullfrog instead of prophet when you hear the word *Jeremiah* . . .

- If you've ever wondered if Mary was a Revised Standard Virgin . . .
- If you think Peter and Paul invented the Almond Joy Bar . . .

Lord knows we can use more than a little humor as we get ready for another meeting of the General Assembly. In light of this, I want to share something ahead of time. With a modest apology to Robert Fulghum and his book *All I Really Need to Know I Learned in Kindergarten*, here is my version of *The Truly Important Things in the Life of Faith I Learned in Vacation Bible School and Other Places in the Church*.

- God is in charge—always has been and always will be—which means that nothing we humans do that is contrary to God's intentions for this world will last. God rules and God overrules our foolishness. God's love overshadows our sinfulness.
- Jesus truly loves me and you and all of us, a truth that has been best communicated to me through relationships—which means that as I experience God's forgiveness through others, I will express it. And as I receive encouragement, I will offer it. Forgiveness and encouragement and correction and all the blessings of Christ's love are best understood by how we relate to one another.
- The Bible tells God's story better than any other book we have, and no matter how much we dig and research and study and wrestle with what it means for our lives . . . or we argue and selectively read and occasionally beat each other with it to prove some point . . . none of that can take away the power of the greatest story ever told!
- Sin is real whether accidental or on purpose, and the human mind is capable of convincing itself that our mean-spirited sinfulness was only accidental or for a good purpose, which means that honesty is always the best policy with God and each other, and truth-telling about ourselves is always the order of the day.

- There is evil in this world, but more often than not, we are the bearers of it, which means I'd best think twice about my own sin because it not only can estrange me from God, it may be making it harder for you to know God too, . . . which also means I'd best be humble before I start pointing out how "evil" your sin is to me.
- Ideas are important, but people matter more. God expects us to treat each other with respect, honesty, and compassion, which means that we must be bold enough to go to people in their hurt and pain . . . and not run away from those whom we don't like because we don't agree with them. We may dismiss another person's ideas but we had best not dismiss him or her.
- Prayer is one of the best change agents we have. Occasionally prayer changes the people and world around us (those are God's miracles); more often, our prayers change ourselves and help us re-center and refocus our lives on the Holy (and that's God's Spirit at work)!

In times of confusion, stress, uncertainty, conflict, we all lean toward some basic ideas and beliefs that steady us and keep us grounded. So, what are yours?

What are the guiding ideas in your life as a Christian? Name the things you have learned that form the foundation of your faith and life. And, who do you count on to help you remember them? Share your own list of the things you learned in Sunday School . . .

15

Education Anyone?

September 1996

The church in this country was built on a three-legged mission that started worshipping communities, hospitals and schools. In Oklahoma, there was a group of Presbyterian leaders with a passion to reform the state's public education system. They successfully worked to pass new laws and then their presbytery encouraged congregations to adopt local schools and so help the children in their communities.

―◊―

Some of you may recall a global conference on world population that was held in Cairo, Egypt, two years ago (1994). I remember listening to a radio program on the conference that summarized the key debate among our sociologists and scientists. You've heard me say before that the world population is expected to double in the next fifty years, from six to twelve billion people.

The key debate is whether or not there is a limit to the number of people our planet can support. It's called the carrying capacity of the earth. Some of our scientists now estimate that we will reach the earth's limit of sixteen to eighteen billion people within the next one hundred years. They argue that the population growth rate must be slowed by both direct laws (such as those in China) and indirect incentives (such as eliminating tax credits for children). Other voices take the position that there isn't a population problem. Unlike other species that have faced crises of overpopulation or extinction, human beings have repeatedly demonstrated an ability to adjust to the changing home we call earth. For example, automobiles today pollute half as much as they did in the 1970s. We've learned how to take worthless things and make them work for us. Crude oil was once considered a nuisance until a Yale University professor figured out how to make kerosene from it. The two inventions that are driving today's information highway, the silicon chip and the fiber-optic cable, are both made from an abundant and "worthless" resource: sand.

With the challenges of a world with twice as many people, the importance of an educated mind becomes all the more important. Those who have the best education will also have the best chance to help our world solve its many problems. My own educational journey from a public school in Ohio, a private Presbyterian college in North Carolina, and a theological seminary in Pennsylvania were foundational and I am so grateful for their many gifts. It makes me think about those who were part of my education: my parents, my teachers and professors, my pastors and youth leaders. And then I remember people I've never met, mostly Presbyterians, who contributed to my schooling by establishing that North Carolina college and underwrote the work of that Pennsylvania seminary so that, in the end, tuition was affordable.

The result has been a strong sense of gratitude. I'm grateful for those who nurtured an appreciation for learning, especially those in the church. I'm grateful for those today who keep teaching me, including my colleagues in ministry. I'm grateful to be part of the Presbyterian Church with its roots clearly set in a love of learning and a willingness to embrace the creative tension that happens when faith and knowledge engage one another. You know our story. We Presbyterians were among the ones who started schools as we settled the west, as were most of the mainline denominations. We endowed scholarships and understood that we had a call from God to foster the learned mind, to nurture the best and brightest and to care for them and provide for them. This commitment is our heritage.

Today our commitment to education has waned. The debates about public schools are complex. The issues are multilayered. The politics can be ugly sometimes. We seem to have divested ourselves from any sense of responsibility when we turned our mission schools over to the public trust. As the same time, the cost of supporting our colleges pales in comparison to our available mission dollars, and the temptation is to turn away from the challenges facing our educational institutions.

In spite of these realities, this presbytery has pursued a dream of improving our public schools through the Education Action Months we've sponsored, the conferences we've held, and the planning books we've written. Nearly half of our congregations have adopted a local school and become involved in mentoring programs and after-school tutoring. Perhaps our schools will improve as we rekindle our commitment to them. Perhaps we will look at the infants we baptize and understand that to teach them means a commitment not only to our Sunday Schools but also to our nation's schools. Perhaps we will look upon the youth who attend our retreats and mission trips as the young people who are counting on us to help them secure the best education possible, because their, and our, future depends on it. The dream is that we will roll up our sleeves to work with our teachers, administrators, and students, that we will share our resources not only for camp scholarships but also for school scholarships, that we will pay attention and expect the best schools in our communities because every child, rich or poor, Presbyterian or not, deserves the opportunity to develop God's most precious gift: his or her mind.

One of John Calvin's more foolish and visionary thoughts was that the church can alter the course of society for the common good. No part of our society needs our attention more than our schools. Presbyterians, among others, did it once. We can do it again.

EDUCATION ANYONE?

This reflection was written before the series of high-profiled school shootings that have happened over the last fifteen years. How has this tragic development made your neighborhood schools more visible to your faith community and if so, what is your leadership team doing to help?

16

The Two-Party View of the Church

December 1996

Jesus said, "Whoever is not with me is against me, and whoever does not gather with me scatters" (Matt 12:30). As the conflicts of the 1990s persisted, I saw this passage used by those on the far edges of the theological spectrum to defend their stridency. How to help people remember that Jesus welcomed all? By remembering a comment from my grandmother.

Every now and then when I travel, I'll turn on some late-night television show, and if I'm lucky, I'll catch a rerun of one of the best television comedies every produced: M*A*S*H. It was a great show and the characters were, and still are, a joy to watch. Here was a group of people thrown together, facing a hostile environment, finding themselves in one stressful moment after another. And most of the time, the sides were clear: Hawkeye and Trapper versus Frank and Charles and Margaret. The arguments, whether they centered on who was in charge or the best way to triage a patient, were usually heated and the tricks they played on each other were mostly silly. But beneath it all you could see the evidence of

The Two-Party View of the Church

their common bonds: that the unit worked and in the end, respect and friendship grew. It was a great show.

The church, from the local congregations to the larger church, looks more and more like a M*A*S*H unit these days. We certainly live in troubled times. There's a lot of hostility around us. We've been thrown together, some would say by the grace of God. We clearly have a job to do. And we have our share of arguments at all levels of our church, enough so that there is an uncomfortable edge about life together. Some of our arguments are more strategic, such as the best way to carry out our mission. Others are more basic, such as who controls the church's decisions. And when some difference erupts into a public feud, there is a tendency to interpret what's happening in terms of the two-party view of the church.

The two-party view of the church says that there are only two basic points of view, and the choices we face are simply yes or no, for or against, either/or. There are segregationists or integrationists, exclusionists or inclusionists, liberals or conservatives, modernists or fundamentalists. Most of the time, however, life is not that simple. Nor are God's people. I first learned this from my Grandma Myrtle. A daughter of the manse, Grandma was a Southern Baptist. She read her Bible every day, said her prayers, took me to her church, and gave me a first glimpse of a committed Christian life. She also gave me my first sip of beer. Oh, she didn't drink much, but she liked her beer on her back porch on a summer evening. When I finally asked about this, she laughed and said, "Oh honey, there's a beer-drinking Baptist in all of us."

While that may not be literally true, her bit of folk wisdom says something about the two-party view of life. In the important decisions the church has recently faced, most of the people involved did not fall into one of two camps. There are more complex dynamics at work in such moments: dynamics that help us value some things on each side of the debate and keep most folks in a middle ground. There may not be a beer-drinking Baptist in us, but very few of us are completely conservative or completely liberal about everything. Few of us are entirely fundamentalist or entirely modernist. For most of us, we're traditionalist about some matters but quite open to change about others. We read some Scripture passages literally, and others contextually. What's missing in the two-party view is the recognition of a center that acknowledges how complex, sometimes confusing and always challenging life and life's choices can be.

A year ago, the Lilly Endowment funded a project that examined this issue. The project was called "Re-Forming the Center." A group of noted church leaders, Martin Marty, George Marsden, and Robert Wuthnow among them, were brought together to consider the premise that a two-party view of church history is inadequate. They concluded that there is a center in the church that can be identified in three ways.

1. Those who find themselves in the center are people who welcome others with a different point of view. While some people can't stand disagreement, those in the center are quite open to hearing a perspective that's different than their own.

2. Those who find themselves in the center find it hard to reduce all thinking to one view or one voice. A centrist is comfortable listening to a variety of voices which all seek to state a common truth.

3. Finally, people who find themselves in the center tend to look at others as friends. They value differences and resist being drawn into the two-party divisions where enemies are so often named.

Frankly, most people in the church are happily centrists. Contrary to radio talk show hosts, most people who feel passionately about some issue are hesitant to name those with whom they disagree as the enemy. Most people in the church want to make room for one another, to listen and to learn, to be respectful and to do as Jesus instructed: to love one another as I have loved you (John 15). And I think most people in the church, even the ones who feel adversarial about some cause, desire to be friends. Friends in Christ. Friends who are patient with each other, friends who respond to God's gracious love with a full measure of grace in their relationships.

What are we letting frame our disagreements: a two-party view of life? Or the love of Jesus Christ? When we shut our eyes for the last time in this life's journey, it really won't matter what we have called ourselves: fundamentalist, liberal, evangelical, centrist. What matters is what happened when we engaged someone with whom we disagreed. Like Hawkeye and B. J. and Charles and Margaret, we're going to disagree and those disagreements will be sharply contrasted at times. What matters, what has always mattered and what will continue to matter is whether or not we received others for the Christian friends they are. What matters is that after our votes are taken, we can say that respect and friendship grew among us, not more bitterness and hostility.

Think about times when you've found yourself in the middle, understanding and partially agreeing with two different perspectives. What gift did you bring to the moment? What fear made you hesitate about remaining in the middle? In the life of your leadership team, where do you see those in the middle having a hard time finding their "voice"? Making a contribution? And what can your leadership team do to make the middle more visible?

17

Sailing on Choppy Seas

June 1997

My sailing experiences have reshaped my basic image of the church. Instead of the church being a lighthouse built on solid ground, the church became a sailboat riding the waters. With the General Assembly having voted to propose another controversial change to our constitution, I knew we had another year of rough waters ahead.

So, a retired Methodist minister stood up at a local lunch gathering of colleagues and introduced himself by saying, "I was born a Methodist, raised a Methodist, retired a Methodist and I'll be buried a Methodist." As he was sitting down, the Presbyterian stood, turned to his neighbor and said in a Scottish accent: "Hoot mon, have you got no ambition?"

A riddle: What did Jesus say to the highway department road crew? Answer: Don't do anything until I get back.

In April, Marney and I took a special anniversary trip, chartering a sailboat in the Caribbean. Along with another couple from seminary days, we four went bareboat chartering, which means there is no skipper or crew to help. Now, the charter company provided a checkout skipper who was to watch us sail the boat for about an hour. The checkout skipper was a Frenchman named Jude and his English was only a little better than my French—which is one word, "Bon!" So, we raised the sail, tacked a few times, set the anchor, took Jude ashore, and headed out.

The next three hours are indelibly marked in my memory. There were choppy seas that afternoon, the swells were three to four feet, and we were making slow progress toward our goal for the night. All this is not good news when you're just getting your sea legs and you haven't bothered to put on one of those seasickness patches. About thirty minutes into our trip, one of us didn't make it and started retching over the side of the boat. The waves and current kept tossing us and there was no place to hide. Going below made matters worse. Motion sickness comes from a disorientation of the inner ear. We later learned that it helps to focus your eyes on some non-moving landmark, to set your sights on some distant object. Eventually, we made it to a safe anchorage and the rest of our trip was outstanding!

As I flew home last week from this year's General Assembly, my sailing trip came back to me. The assembly has voted to send another amendment to the constitution that modifies last year's Amendment B about the fidelity and chastity of church officers. It's no stretch to suggest that our church is being tossed to and fro, one year this way and the next year that way. And how many of us are suffering a bit of motion sickness? Or retching a bit over the side of our boat? The church is being driven by the Spirit's winds in ways I don't fully understand and we're riding the currents and waves of a culture that aren't always predictable. There aren't many choices but to ride it out. We can't turn the boat around, we have to ride with the wind. We ought to pause before jumping ship because the sea can be unfriendly and most every other denominational boat I know is travelling through similarly choppy waters.

Then a bit of peace came to me: I remembered that we Presbyterians know how to ride these choppy waters. We can let God's Spirit do the leading. We can feel for our friends and ourselves experiencing the motion sickness, the pain or disappointment, and try to be helpful and comforting. Living within the realm of God's peace is possible if we remember to keep our sights focused on the destination: God's kingdom coming among us. God's mountain, God's city, God's redeeming love in Christ. It's not clear exactly where the winds are taking us, but we can be at peace that God will help find a safe landfall for us together.

Last week's lectionary reading was the story of Jesus calming the storm. One of the sermons I heard last Sunday had linked Mark 4 to the 46th Psalm, a reminder of who's in charge and to whom we belong and the one whom we can trust:

> God is our refuge and strength, a very present help in trouble
> Therefore we will not fear though the earth should change,
> Though the mountains shake in the heart of the sea
> Though its waters roar and foam, though the mountains tremble with its tumult
> There is a river whose streams make glad the city of God
> The holy habitation of the Most High
> God is in the midst of the city; it shall not be moved;
> God will help it when the morning dawns
> The nations are in an uproar, the kingdoms totter; he utters his voice, the earth melts.
> The Lord of hosts is with us; the God of Jacob is our refuge.
> Be still and know that I am God! I am exalted among the nations, I am exalted in the earth. The Lord of hosts is with us; the God of Jacob is our refuge.

Recall a recent storm faced by your leadership team. What actions helped to calm the stormy emotions and remind you of the shore and your destination?

18

Anticipating the Next Millennium

March 1998

My first report in a new position as general presbyter of Grace Presbytery (Dallas / Fort Worth / NE Texas) coincided with the growing public awareness that the year 2000 was fast approaching.

———◇———

January 1, the year 2000, is 657 days from today, and with it, a new millenium will begin. I don't know if you caught the news story, but last April 6th, to mark the final thousand days before the next thousand years, one thousand musicians in the New York area gathered themselves into the Times Square All Star Millennium Marching Band and held a parade. Leave it to New Yorkers, I suppose. A new millennium is upon us. It's all around us. There's the Millennia car, the Millennia perfume, and the candy of the new millennium, M&Ms. Have you made your plans for December 31st, 1999? Disney World is already booked.

It's a bit arbitrary, this marking of the passage of time, but as it nears, I suspect it will gain increasing significance. One of those New York band members, a fifteen-year-old high school student and a member of the Class of 2000, commented on why this date is important to her: "People will look back on us. We must do our best," she said. "The hard part is knowing how."

I want to pose a simple question to you: For all of the new mission designs and staffing plans Grace Presbytery has been shaping, do you think we'll be any different when the new millennium begins? More specifically, in what ways will we be challenging our congregations to energetically explore the mission frontier that is right outside their doors? Will we be providing leadership to the whole church as God's generous stewards, or as God's passionate evangelists, or as God's advocates for justice and peace?

As I think about a new beginning for me in the continuing journey of Grace Presbytery, it occurs to me to say two things. First, our readiness to lead in the future depends on how tightly we will weave the fabric of this body; that is, the relationships we have with each other. Whatever else the Book of Order may say about our identity and responsibility, we are first an expression of the community of Jesus Christ. The weaving of those relationships takes time and energy, commitment and openness, nurturing friendships that span our political and theological and cultural/racial differences. As with your congregation, Grace Presbytery is a community where our relationships are best nurtured through worship, prayer, witness and service.

The second thing that occurs to me to say is that our readiness to lead the church into a new millennium depends on how well we let go of the assumptions that keep us rooted in the past. We are in a time of change. God's leading the way and calling us into a future not yet known. I suspect that facing that future will require our letting go of some assumptions from the past. Of who does what: staff, elders, ministers. Of how we get things done, as in we've always done it this way.

Neither of these thoughts is new. We know these things to be true. So allow me to ask: if, over the next 657 days, we ministers sit in our respective offices and don't broaden the reach of our friendships, and if we elders sit in our respective pews and don't visit each others' churches, and if all of us simply come to these meetings and sit with the same old friends we've been sitting with for years, do you think we'll be any different when January 1st, 2000, arrives? Do you think we'll have any more to offer to our church?

"People will look back on us. We must do our best. The hard part is knowing how." As a leadership team what is the "moment" you are facing? What attitudes and actions will reflect your "bringing your best"?

19

Nurturing Disciples

September 1998

During the Twentieth Century, there was a significant change in the word used to identify the individuals who participated in our congregations. "Disciples" was replaced with "members." To refocus the church's mission, a growing number of leaders were returning to the language of "disciples."

It has been exciting to see the energy generated by our theological discussion this past hour. Among the most important marks of the church is our willingness to place our business decisions in the context of our theology. And that requires more than simply an opening and closing prayer. It requires a continual attentiveness to the Word, a use of the language of God, and a commitment to filter life's events through the eyes of faith.

To illustrate the importance of our priorities, the leader of a time management workshop once set a one-gallon, wide-mouth mason jar on a table. Then she produced a dozen fist-sized rocks and carefully placed them into the jar. When she couldn't fit anymore inside, she asked, "Is the jar full?" The class answered "yes."

"No," she replied, and then produced a small bucket of gravel. She dumped some in and shook the jar so that the pieces filled all the spaces between the big rocks. Again she asked, "Is the jar full?" This time the class answered, "probably not."

"Good," she said, and then produced some sand and dumped the sand into the jar. The class watched as the sand filled the spaces between the rocks and gravel. Once more, she asked, "Is the jar full?" "No," they replied.

"Correct," she said as she then poured water into the jar until it was filled to the brim. "Now, what's the point?" she asked. One of the participants offered. "No matter how full your schedule is, if you try really hard, you can always fit one more thing into it."

"No," the leader replied. "The truth is that you have to put the big rocks in first, or you'll never get them in at all."

This illustration addresses more than our personal management of time. It speaks to the life and time we spend in the church. I suspect we all find ourselves at some point or another, spending too much time on the pebbles and the sand in our "church jars" and then discovering that there isn't time for the important big rocks. Invest your time in your priorities. Deal with the big rocks first.

So, what would you call the "big rocks" in your church: the tasks, the ministries, the emphases that need to be addressed first because they are the more important things. The rocks, I suppose, could be our programs—worship, church school, new member classes. They could be ideas—such as knowledge of the Scriptures, the marks of church membership, or the principles of church government. What are the big rocks you'd choose for your congregation's jar?

I encourage you to include the "nurturing of disciples" on your list of the big rocks. We would do well to set a goal of helping every person claim a clearer sense of discipleship to Jesus Christ, both inside the church and in everyday life: in the home and family life, in the workplace, and the marketplace.

Ask the grocery store cashier about her faith, as she offers a smile to her customers, not because it's good for business but rather because she understands it as her ministry: to bring a little light into the lives of those hassled and hurried people who pass through her line each day. Or, ask the owner of Tom's of Maine, a business executive whose faith has led him to operate a healthcare products company that is both environmentally sensitive and profitable for all his employees. These are the kind of disciples whose faith needs the nurturing of the church.

How do we do this? By inviting every member to rediscover and reaffirm his or her calling into the world. By affirming people in their vocational callings and helping them claim how God has led them to their chosen work. By exploring the link between our baptism and our vocation, wherein the one—as the claiming and blessing of God in our lives—leads to the other, our response in ministry. By broadening the use of the word "ministry" to include the work of all the saints in their daily lives and not just their Sunday lives.

The church in God's future will find ways to do all of this. It will lift up baptism not only as an event that happens once, but as a lens through which we see and live the rest of our lives. The church of God's future will see itself as a center of education that prepares its lay members for their daily ministries. It will provide support for these lay ministries both in the sermons and the small groups that are gathered. What is your church doing to nurture the disciples in your congregation? What more might you do? How might this presbytery help?

The institutional church often asks what its members can do for the church. Now it is being called to focus more on what the church can do for Christ's disciples. How has this change impacted your leadership team and community of faith?

20

A Vision

Discipleship, Leadership, Partnership, Mission

May 1999

This particular report presented a vision for the presbytery and its congregations. It was offered a year after I began my service to Grace Presbytery, and became a defining moment in my service there.

———◆———

Mr. Moderator, Members and Commissioners: Recently, I came across a list of the top oxymorons in the church: No. 6, pastor's day off; No. 5, early sign-up; No. 4, clear calendar; No. 3, volunteer waiting list; No. 2, realistic budget; No. 1, concluding remarks. Now, I don't mean to disappoint. There will be a concluding remark in this report, but not just yet!

This coming Sunday, pending our vote later this morning, we will organize a new church (the Southlake Blvd. Presbyterian Church) and the 186th congregation of Grace Presbytery. This is the first new church to be granted a charter in two years. With three more new church developments currently holding worship services, Sunday's celebration is both the fulfillment of one dream and a promise of things to come.

How appropriate for this to take place on Pentecost Sunday. In last week's issue of the "Presbyterian Outlook," editor Robert Bullock reflected:

> The miracle of Pentecost is that the word of God was proclaimed by the apostles and that it was heard and understood by citizens of many nations. The church of the risen Lord was born. Pentecost stands in contrast to Babel, where the language of the proud was confused and their works defeated by the judgment of God.

In assessing the current state of the church, Robert says that a key underlying issue is our failure to communicate—to use words in such a way that draws us together rather than sends us into enclaves and isolation. He concludes that when it becomes harder and harder for us to talk to one another, we need to pray for a fresh outpouring of the Holy Spirit on our church.

Over the years, I have come to understand that one of the other gifts of the Spirit is vision. One sign of the very real presence of God in our lives is our ability to state what we understand God wants for us and hopes for us. Vision can be elusive, but when people have a picture of where God would have them go, they come alive in focused and determined ways. The biblical proverb about vision is true: where there is no vision, the people perish, and the scriptures are filled with stories of people seeking and claiming God's vision for them. Most often, it is the work of leaders who make this happen. First, leaders must be in touch with the vision that guides their own work and service. Second, they need to have good questions for the people to encourage them in this work. Third, they need to offer those images which prompt others' curiosity and imagination.

In light of this, there are two comments I'd make about Grace Presbytery. The first is that I continue to be impressed by the vision that has shaped its life and current structure, priorities, programs. As associate executives, Rick Carus, Wilson Gunn, Janine Wilson and I continue to visit our congregations and work with the council, we see a presbytery vision that has four elements: (1) to support our congregations with some basic programs and

A Vision

individual assistance; (2) to support our church professionals, encouraging excellence and collegiality in their service; (3) to extend the church's reach by starting new congregations and by redeveloping others; and (4) to undergird all this with the most effective resource network of people and technology that we can assemble. Behind this vision is the hope that our life and work will reflect the communal and covenantal values of respect and care. It's a vision good enough to have redirected this presbytery's journey some years ago, and remembering just how slow and sometimes resistant organizations can be in their transformation, it's good enough to hold onto for the time being.

The second thing I want to say is that it's not enough. It's not enough for Grace Presbytery to have a dream for only its future—a vision for its own life. The presbytery must also claim a vision for the congregations entrusted to its care. Our presbytery needs to have a sense of how our congregations can best prepare for the next twenty-five, thirty, fifty years, and then encourage them in those ways.

How are we going to help our congregations fulfill the great ends of the church in the next century? The next millenium? Given all of the changes going on around us (in this country, in our Western culture, in the world) and given all of the challenges (both the good promises and the fearful worries) of the future, how can we help our congregations? By being bold enough, humble enough, and passionate enough to share our vision with them—of what we must do next to fulfill the great ends that we continue to claim as Presbyterians.

And this is precisely where I want to invite you to join the Presbytery Council in a conversation as pastors and specialized ministers, as retirees, as educators, as elders. I want to begin the conversation by lifting up four elements of the church's life that I believe need our immediate and sustained attention. I believe these four can help us focus on the truly important work of the church and can be summed up in the words: discipleship, leadership, partnership, mission. Scriptures speak to all four of these and history attests that when the church has been attentive to them, it has thrived. Discipleship, Leadership, Partnership, Mission.

By *discipleship*, I mean the work that nurtures each individual believer in the life of faith. We must do more to nurture, celebrate, and encourage the personal discipleship of every member—baptized, gifted and called by God. On the close of this twentieth century, it's time we face the reality that: (a) too many people in our congregations don't read, study, or know how to incorporate the Scriptures into their living; (b) too many people in our congregations don't know how to pray, be good stewards, be disciplined in their life of faith; (c) too many people in our congregations don't see the connect between their faith and their lives in the workplace, marketplace, and sometimes even the home place. Congregations that emphasize discipleship at the center of the ministry to their members will be offering a great gift to the church.

The *leadership* issue is critical because we are living in a time when people demand that leaders bring immediate and direct results, and yet expect that every one who is affected by some decision has a part in making it. We ordain officers, some of whom have been Presbyterians for a brief period of time, and we expect them to absorb our Presbyterian heritage and commitment to a covenantal and communal life in the annual officers' retreat. We ordain ministers and set them into places where impatience and institutional anxiety distracts them from the work of pursuing and enabling spiritual growth and lifelong learning in themselves and others. The church needs leaders who know the basics and are open to trying new ways of being the church, and the congregations that emphasize the spiritual and leadership development of ministers, educators, officers and others will do well in the coming years.

Partnership is basic to Presbyterianism. In the past, we counted on the denomination to shape our partnerships. That's no longer true. Today, there are three partnerships that fall on the shoulder of every Presbyterian congregation to develop: a denominational partnership with other Presbyterians; an ecumenical partnership with other Christians nearby; and an international partnership

A Vision

with Christians in other places of the world. All of them are needed as ways of broadening our view of how the church is working and can work for us. It is not enough to sit back and wait for others to engage us; we must take the initiative. Congregations that invest themselves in strengthening these kinds of partnerships will be better prepared to minister amidst the continual changes affecting all of us.

Finally, the word *mission* is not that broad umbrella under which all forms of ministry can be placed, but rather that more focused work of finding people in our neighborhoods and communities who need some help, and then helping them for the love of God. Whether we're talking about the work of compassion or the work of justice, there are simply too many people being hurt by being ignored or treated unfairly. There are too many folks in some kind of need and it isn't enough for us to simply offer worship services, potluck meals and Bible studies, or write a check. Most congregations that go searching for a place to serve won't have far to look, I suspect, and they will discover energy and meaning in their service.

Discipleship, leadership, partnership, mission. I believe that congregations that place special emphasis on these four will go well into the coming years. Such a vision for our congregations has the potential to influence the life of this Presbytery. If this were to be the vision we'd claim for our congregations, then it would impact the goals we set and the programs we offer—for example, making sure our summer camp and youth programs nurture discipleship and encourage leadership development. It would impact the way we start new churches. It would impact which redeveloping congregations we fund. It could impact which Mission Initiative grants we award.

Discipleship, leadership, partnership, mission: I invite you to consider these as a starting place for a conversation we would do well to have all across the presbytery. At Council's urging, these ideas have been developed into a study paper. It's being offered along with a prayer for a fresh outpouring of the Holy Spirit as we talk, pray and direct our efforts in the coming days.

Standing in front of the other members of your leadership team, what would be the key ideas you would offer as your vision for the near future?

21

Editorial

Peace, Unity, Purity

March 2002

Paul writes in his first letter to the church in Corinth: "Now we see in a mirror dimly, but then we shall see face to face" (13:12). Humility and hope come to mind as I think about these words of Scripture and apply them to a particularly nagging problem in the church.

The questions we ask when anyone is ordained to the office deacon, ruling elder, or teaching elder are sacred, profound, and challenging. When I moderate an ordination or installation service for a new minister in the presbytery, I find that the most difficult question to ask is: "Do you promise to further the peace, unity and purity of the church?" The question is difficult because peace, unity and purity create a tension that is hard to ignore and hard to live with. And it's difficult because it is not a multiple choice question (pick one of them); it is not an either/or choice (either peace or purity, either unity or purity, etc.). Somehow, our forebears had the wisdom to put before those of us who are ordained the challenge to uphold the peace *and* the unity *and* the purity of the church.

- Peace, not the absence of tension, but the presence of justice
- Unity, not uniformity, but a oneness where what unites us far exceeds what divides us
- Purity, both in belief—orthodoxy—and practice—orthopraxis

Several questions come to mind: How are we to emphasize all three of these in a balanced way? Can we focus too much attention on one to the point that the others suffer? Are we to understand that at some times in our history, one is more important to emphasize than the others and therefore we let them go by the wayside? Is it possible to be fully at peace, united and pure as the people of God? How do we pay attention to all three, even when it often feels that they are mutually exclusive? The fact is that to be *completely* united means our purity will suffer. To be *completely* pure in doctrine/practice means our unity will suffer.

To promise to *further* all three of these means that we must not ever emphasize one of them so much that we completely lose touch with the other two. I wish I knew how to do this perfectly. Right now I see this dimly. One day . . .

In the meantime, I choose to live humbly and hopefully and I will keep working to honor this most challenging of our ordination questions: do you promise to further the *peace, unity* and *purity* of the church?

Which of these three (peace, unity, purity) is it easiest for you to embrace? Which is the hardest? What about for your leadership team?

22

A Spirituality of Unity

November 2002

In a season when we spend too much time aware of the differences among Christians, it is a blessing to have some moments when Christian unity is honored. One of those moments happened as I was introduced to the Focolare Movement, founded after World war II in Italy and Germany. Bishop Charles Grahmann (Honorably Retired), of the Roman Catholic Diocese of Dallas, invited several of us to join him for the 2002 annual Bishops meeting of the Focolare when it took place in Geneva, Switzerland.

———◦———

Several weeks ago, I was introducing myself at an ecumenical gathering with the religious litany that many of you have heard me recount: My mother was Baptist, my father Jewish, I was raised a Methodist, and then married an Episcopalian . . . and before I could finish, someone piped up, "So that's how you become a Presbyterian!" "Not always," I replied, "some of us are born this way."

The meeting I was attending was being held outside Geneva, Switzerland, and the participants came from Asia, North and South America, Europe and the Middle East. We were Catholic, Anglican, Orthodox, Reformed. We were not gathered by the

World Council of Churches, but rather by an eighty-two-year-old Catholic laywoman. This was the twenty-fifth Bishops Meeting in support of the Focolare Movement.

Every now and then we have experiences that open our eyes to how small the world is and how richly complex is its human tapestry. The bishops, archbishops, and three of us executives gathered for a week of prayer, sharing, study, and all in support of a fifty-year-old lay movement that is being built upon the unity of Jesus Christ. That week, I met a Cuban Presbyterian who is now the Anglican Bishop of Uruguay. I prayed with a German who has been the Catholic Bishop of Norway for over seventeen years. I shared stories with a Brit who was raised Jewish, bar-mitzvahed, then converted to Christianity and became an Anglican bishop. I received a blessing from a cardinal who, during the years of Communist control in Czechoslovakia, had to wash windows as his "meaningful" work. I laughed with an Orthodox bishop from, of all places, Cochin, India, in the state of Kerala, where our partnership with the Church of South India resides. On a Sunday morning, we worshipped in the Cathedral of Calvin's Reformation, St. Peters, where the current president of the Reformed Church in Geneva is a French Mennonite and the dean of the cathedral is an Irishman. That day, over two thousand gathered in this church of the Reformation, many of them young people in their twenties and thirties, to listen to this eighty-two-year-old, blue-haired lady.

Chiara Lubich, an Italian, is the founder of the Focolare Movement. The word means warmth or hearth. It is one of the few lay Catholic orders recognized by Rome. In the bomb shelters of Trent, Italy, during World War II, she caught a glimpse of the gospel that has moved her and millions of others to commit their lives to unity in Christ, to the oneness that lies at the heart of gospel. Watching their youthful hopes and dreams of careers and families vanish under the shower of bombs, they asked: Is there anything in this life that doesn't vanish? Their answer was God. God's love does not vanish. From this, they have built an ecumenical presence where their members: (a) look first to find Jesus in their midst in those around them; (b) remember the forsakenness of Jesus on the cross and reach out to love those who are experiencing forsakenness in their lives; and (c) love their neighbors with prayer and acts of kindness. For those who commit themselves to the Order of the Focolare, they take Jesus' words seriously about friends being willing to lay down their lives for the other. For the Focolare, these are the disciplines that nurture the unity of Christ's body.

This spirituality of unity captures the basics of the gospel I think. Simply stated: (a) God is love; (b) God's love endures and can be relied upon; (c) we are to look for Jesus present in the other person; (d) we are to love God and love our neighbors; and (e) lay down our life for our friends. It's both pragmatic and idealistic. So then, on Sunday morning, I wake up and join the Anglicans and Lutherans for a prayer service in a basement chapel that makes me think of the catacombs, and later worship in a cathedral of the Reformation where a Catholic laywoman preaches, and end my day attending a Catholic Eucharist, where I receive a blessing but am not invited to the table. The realities of our differences aren't set aside. Rather, they are recognized as moments of Jesus being forsaken.

What does Jesus want? Does he want the forsakenness? Does he want us to focus on all the ways we have yet to be reconciled? Or, does he want the unity of his body? Does he want us to submit ourselves to his unity by recognizing his presence among us and acknowledging all that we have in common through God's love?

A spirituality of unity has something to say to worldwide Christendom—to Orthodox, Catholic, Reformed and the independent churches. It was not by chance that this meeting took place in Geneva—the World Council of Churches is seeking to learn more about the unity of the Focolare. What strikes me is that a spirituality of unity probably has something to say to the Presbyterian Church, too. It isn't going to happen because we simply wish it, or pray for it. It will happen as we pursue the disciplines that nurture the unity of the body.

God is love. God wants us to love others. We must look for Jesus in the other. We must reach out in concrete ways when the other is going through the pain of feeling forsaken and lost. And we would do well to look in the face of the other and ask, "Would I give my life so that this other person could be a full and faithful person of Christ?"

It's one thing to be respectful and polite about our differences. But if we want to be truly great for Christ's sake, then we would do well to commit ourselves to the disciplines of such a spirituality, where we pray for the other and truly want the best for the other one, and will work together to make it happen.

What might you be doing to nurture our oneness of Jesus Christ? In your community? Among other religious communities?

23

Editorial

Basic Tenets of the Faith

February 7, 2003

In recent months, there has been increasing talk about a new crisis in our church. In addition to the membership crisis, the monetary crisis, and the constitutional crisis, is what some are calling a "confessional crisis." The disagreements we experience over the nature of God, the authority of Scripture and the saving work of Jesus Christ threaten our ability to find common theological ground. We are a church with multiple confessional documents, and different groups among us favor one particular confession, or selectively emphasize different parts of several confessions. In addition, an increasing number of congregations are joining para-confessional movements such as the More Light Churches or the Confessing Churches.

It's quite fair to ask, "Is there anything we Presbyterians share besides the basic confession that Jesus Christ is Lord?" Are there any basic beliefs that we all hold? Consider the following:

1. We Presbyterians agree with all Christians that God is three (Father, Son, Holy Spirit) in one. We are Trinitarian, not

Unitarian. The Trinity is Mystery: we can't fully understand it, and no analogy can fully explain it. Yet we believe it.

2. We Presbyterians agree with all Christians that God came to the world in the flesh in Jesus Christ. Jesus, fully human and fully God. We can't fully understand it, and no analogy can fully explain it. Yet we believe it.

3. We Presbyterians agree with Protestant Christians that the Scriptures of the Old and New Testaments offers the authoritative word about salvation and the life of faith. Whatever we may come to believe based on our personal experiences and whatever authority we may give to the church's proclamations must be tested against the truthfulness of the Scriptures. People of good faith may disagree on how to interpret Scripture. Even so, God's Word in Scripture is authoritative.

4. We Presbyterians agree with most Protestant Christians that our salvation cannot be earned. It is God's gracious gift alone. And it is faith alone, not good deeds, that opens the door to God's saving love. That's called being justified by faith. We can't fully understand it and no analogy can fully explain it. Yet we believe it.

5. We Presbyterians agree with other Reformed Christians that God is sovereign. God is good all the time; all the time God is good. In the world in which we live, and in the way we live in the world, God rules and overrules our foolishness. Even when there's a crisis, God's rule and not our disagreements, desires, or intentions will prevail. Period.

6. We Presbyterians agree with other Reformed Christians that some people out of all the human race are claimed for salvation through Christ and called to a life of witness and service. Whenever anyone joins a Christian church, we believe it to be a sign that God has elected that person for salvation and service. God has brought this person to us. God has chosen this person. And those whom God brings together, let no one separate.

7. We Presbyterians agree with other Reformed Christians that God wants an orderly life for the church; that we are to make agreements, to covenant with God and each other to be a church that is a visible expression of what God has promised is to be the kingdom/realm in its fullness.

8. We Presbyterians believe that one of the greatest sins is idolatry—putting anything above God: any idea, any person, any desire. We worry about this because we don't have to look any farther than ourselves to know how easy it is to put God in second position.

9. We Presbyterians believe that stewardship is a matter of all of life. Everything is a gift from God. When we Presbyterians think about it, we can trace the path of all we have back to God. We're to spend everything God gives to us wisely—our money, our talents, our time—and to do anything less is foolishness.

10. We Presbyterians believe that obedience to the Word of God is not just an individual matter and that salvation is more than something personal. God wants justice and peace in our world, a hard challenge because it is a peace and justice that only God fully understands. Yet God expects us to give ourselves to this work in the world.

This little list comes from the second chapter of our Book of Order, on the confessions. Before we organize our Presbyterian church into congregations, presbyteries, synods and a General Assembly, we make it clear what we believe: Jesus Christ is Lord of all, Head of the Church (chapter 1). And then we Presbyterians declare the core beliefs we hold dear (chapter 2).

As I visit the congregations of our Presbytery, participate in worship, and listen to elders in conversation, I don't hear disagreement over these essentials. Some are discussed more energetically than others, but when the question is asked, no elder or minister I know disclaims any of them. As a confessional church we hold much in common. I thank God for that, and for the way we Presbyterians claim the faith and look at life . . .

... which is not to diminish the importance of our current disagreements, but rather to remind us of the common essentials *from which* we disagree and with God's help, *through which* we may find our path into God's future together.

———◦———

In addition to these tenets, what others parts of our life together do we hold in common?

24

The Missional Church

September 2003

During the opening years of a new century, a growing number of church leaders sensed that the church's institutional life was overshadowing its mission. The result was a church not bearing fruit. So, the missional church initiative became and continues to be important to the renewal of Christ's body.

Three friends from the local congregation were asked, "When you're in your casket and your friends are mourning over you, what would you like them to say?" The first replied, "I'd like them to say I was a wonderful husband and father and church member." The second said, "I'd like them to say I was a good businessman and church leader who made a contribution to Christ's church." The third said, "I'd like them to say, 'Look! He's moving!'"

Our Presbytery Council is getting ready to host four important gatherings next month. There are no decisions to be made. Rather, the council hopes that a conversation will grow among us. And, you are being invited to bring as many from your congregation's leadership groups as you can. The focus of the conversation is the missional church.

To set the stage, the council has asked that I remind you of our story. There was once a time when there was no church. Then when the Holy Spirit was poured out upon Christ's disciples—the first Apostolic Age was born. People shared the good news of Christ. Communities of believers were formed that made a difference in peoples lives. The focus was telling, sharing with people who had not heard about the risen Christ. And more and more people became disciples and joined this new religious movement.

Then Christianity became an official religion. The Roman Emperor Constantine became a believer and mandated Christianity as the official religion of the empire. Over the next sixteen centuries, other empires did the same—the British Empire and the Spanish Empire among them. Wherever the European monarchs sent navies and armies and merchants and colonial administrators, they sent priests and ministers to insure that Christianity was officially introduced and accepted. And so among these other global kingdoms something new emerged: Christendom. And in many ways the church had it easy. Since the masses were being told or at least encouraged to go to church by the government and the culture and the Sunday blue laws, the church focused mostly on what happened inside its doors. Buildings were built, bylaws were written, curriculum was produced, and introducing the faith focused on the children: raising them up inside institutional Christianity. Less and less the church was a people sharing their faith with other people; more and more it became an institution that witnessed to other institutions. And up until about forty years ago, life in the church was pretty straightforward.

Today, more and more church leaders are saying that we are entering a new age for the Christian movement: a new Apostolic Age. Welcome to this time when many of the old ways no longer work, welcome to a time when keeping the traditions appears less important than taking new initiatives to share the faith personally and invite participation in a community of the faith. In this new Apostolic Age, we do well to take some cues from the first one. So get out your history books, open up your Bibles, God seems to have a new thing in mind.

The Missional Church

Among the ideas that have surfaced during this time of change is something called the Missional Church. It's not a formula as much as it is an orientation. The purpose is to think and act missionally, and not institutionally.

Retired Episcopal bishop Claude Payne draws a helpful distinction between the institutional maintenance of the past and the missional initiative of today. He writes:

> [One way] to contrast the First Apostolic Age and the Age of Christendom is in terms of Church models based on focus. The First Apostolic Age was characterized by a model that emphasized community and mission. The Age of Christendom was [more]characterized by a model that emphasized community without mission—that is, maintenance of the status quo. Today's maintenance-centered church primarily serves the faithful, those who are already Christian, were raised a Christian and are expected to die Christian. It is not particularly attentive to the unchurched except [in philosophical ways, paying lip service to the work of evangelism]." (*Reclaiming the Great Commission*, Payne and Beazeley, 2002)

The maintenance-centered church focuses on making members; the mission-centered church is interested in making disciples. The maintenance-centered church budgets for the people already there; the mission-centered church budgets for people not yet there. Maintenance-centered churches do a lot of rule-making; the mission-centered church does more permission-giving.

We find ourselves in a time when a fundamental reorientation of the church's work seems to be what's called for. I don't know how we can do this without gathering together, listening and sharing, and helping one another. It is a significant moment.

In your leadership team's discussions about the church and change, what ideas from the missional church are guiding your thinking? What are the next steps you'd like to see your leadership team take?

25

Editorial

A Different Top Ten

March 2004

In anticipation of each national General Assembly meeting, the Stated Clerk sends out a list of the ten most important items of business: proposed changes to the meeting rules, proposed amendments to the church constitution, special reports to be adopted, social concerns needing addressed. In conversation with regional leaders interested in the Missional Church Initiative, the following list was offered:

To the Commissioners, Delegates and Observers to the 216th (2004) General Assembly:

"You cannot enter the Kingdom of Heaven unless you are born anew" (John 3:3). No one touched by God ever remains the same. In addition to the important decisions our General Assembly commissioner will face, there are deeper issues about our life together they will confront, by God's grace. Among them:

> 10. Will we see the many faces of God, and not just the one we know best?

9. Will we recognize God in the silence, and not just the cacophony of our own making?
8. Will we stand in front of the mirror long enough to see the log in our own eye?
7. Will we remember that we are a son/daughter of a living and loving God?
6. Will we allow God to come close enough that we don't have to shout?
5. Will we cut off the panoply of God's experience by our preference for the immediate and pleasing?
4. Will we patiently sing our laments and not rush to kill the pain?
3. Will we see and celebrate the Holy in our everyday experiences?
2. Will we bring the discipline of listening to our conversations?
1. Will we keep asking, and asking, and asking: What is God's mission? What is my part in God's mission? What is my congregation's role in God's mission? What is our church's (presbytery's, synod's, General Assembly's) place in God's mission?

Which of these questions speaks most to your leadership team's work?

26

Editorial

Reclaiming Time to Think

April 2004

Will we reclaim time to think? This is one of many questions posed by Margaret Wheatley in her book *Turning to One Another: Simple Conversations to Restore Hope to the Future* (Berrett-Koehler, San Francisco, 2002). Wheatley says that it is through conversation we begin to change the world. She tells stories of people making a difference who say, "It all started one day when a friend and I had a conversation . . ." To the particular question of thinking, I'll let her speak directly (pp. 96–99):

> As a species, we humans possess some unique capacities. We can stand apart from what's going on, think about it, question it, imagine it being different. We are also curious. We want to know "why?" We figure out "how?" We think about what's past, we dream forward to the future.
>
> As the world speeds up, we're giving away these wonderful human capacities. Do you have as much time to think as you did a year ago? When was the last time you spent time reflecting on something important to you? Are you encouraged to spend time thinking with

colleagues and co-workers, or reflecting on what you're learning?

To see whether you're losing anything of value to yourself, here are some questions to ask: Are my relationships with those I love improving or deteriorating? Is my curiosity about the world increasing or decreasing? Do I feel more or less energy for my work than a few years ago? Are those things that anger me different than a few years ago? Generally, am I feeling more peaceful or more stressed?

If answering those questions helps you notice anything you'd like to change, you will have to find some time to think about it. But don't expect anybody to give you this time. You will have to claim it for yourself.

Thinking is not inaction. When people can think and notice what's going on, we develop ideas that we hope will improve our lives. As soon as we discover something that might work, we act. When the ideas mean something to us, the distance between thinking and acting dissolves. People don't hesitate to get started. They just start doing. If that action doesn't work, they try something different . . . Most of us don't have to risk life and death daily, but we may be dying a slow death. If we feel we're changing in ways we don't like, or seeing things in the world that make us feel sorrowful, then we need time to think about this. We need time to think about what we might do and where we might start to change things. We need time to develop clarity and courage.

Wheatley concludes, "If we want our world to be different, our first act needs to be reclaiming time to think. Nothing will change for the better until we do that." And so, too, I might add, if we want our church to be different.

One of the bits of wisdom that comes our way if we live long enough is this insight about the difference between doing and thinking, acting and reflecting, the rhythm between action and contemplation.

Is "reclaiming time to think" only a matter for each individual? Can leadership teams claim this value and make the commitment to take more time to think together? What kind of decisions most need your team's thinking?

27

Editorial

Sermons Are Not Fast Food

August 2004

Pardon a rant for a moment. From time to time I hear someone voice one of the more common complaints about pastors: "My pastor's sermons don't speak to me." That's the kinder, gentler version of what is often voiced in church conflicts: "The pastor's a lousy preacher and it's time for him/her to go." Usually by the time I hear this, the pastor is picking up the same signals by the comments or lack of them during the post-worship greeting line on Sundays (usually around high noon, the time of many a Western shootout).

Well, God gives gifts to ministers in a variety of ways. It's true some of our pastors are great preachers, some are not. So what? God can speak through the best of us and God can speak through the worst of us.

I am reminded of Arnold Webster—a horticulturalist Presbyterian from Iowa who was my best sermon critic and encourager in the faith for the five years I served as an associate pastor there. Arnold was a devoted disciple. He said his prayers, read his Bible, and whenever he knew what the upcoming sermon text would be, he read the passage repeatedly during the week beforehand. When he came to worship, Arnold said a prayer for the preacher. Not a prayer that the sermon would be good, but a prayer that God would speak through it. And Arnold always had a kindly word. He had a gentle way of addressing what he saw was a missed opportunity in exegesis or interpretation. And because I knew Arnold was doing his homework and preparing to hear, I found myself willing to listen to this friend in the faith.

The real criticism of the sermon critic is that we don't make it easy for them. We expect our preachers to prepare to preach their sermons. But, what do we expect our parishioners to do to prepare to hear the message? The gospel is to be found in the *hearing* of God's Word and we who sit in the pews miss the mark if we think that the only one who needs to prepare for Sunday's sermon is the one who stands up to speak. Preparing by reading the texts, praying for the preacher, praying the texts, talking with a spouse or friend, connecting other readings and events with the text, even participating in a class. I believe that if each pew sitter spent half the time "preparing to hear" that our preachers spend "preparing to give" a sermon, there'd be a bit more intelligent conversation happening around the "preached word." A bit more grace and gratitude would fill our sanctuaries. We'd have some very different churches in which to gather for worship and praise, and to which to invite others.

In our consumer-oriented society, it is wise to quit seeing sermons the way we see a fast-food chicken sandwich! We all need to be preparing ourselves to hear the Word preached in our gathered communities.

We live under the pressure to do more and more. The unintended consequence is that we have less time to prepare for all this "doing," including the act of listening. Is there a connection in your community between the ones who are most critical and the ones who are least prepared? What might your leadership team do in response?

28

Editorial

Our Witness with Prayer

March 2005

In this Lenten season, I want to reflect on the discipline of prayer. I recently read an article about a mainline Protestant seminary student spending a nine-month internship in a large independent evangelical church. The article included a list of things that mainline Protestants can learn from such independent churches, followed by a list of the things we might teach them.

About prayer at this independent church she wrote: "Nothing happens at this church without the power of prayer surrounding it . . . and supporting it. Every major event of the church is prayed for by a group of people as the event is being held. Public prayer is not the domain of church leadership; responsibility to lead prayer belongs to everyone."

In contrast, most mainline prayers tend to be more formal. Because the language of our prayer is more formal, most people don't feel comfortable leading prayer. The pastor is usually expected to speak, while others pray along quietly. While we don't believe that more people praying equates to better prayers, we count too much on the pastor or one of a few elders to pray publicly.

Most of us don't come from a tradition that has nurtured the public prayers of the laity. And yet, we rebel against those forms of the church that restrict access to God to the priest or pastor.

So, what can we do to overcome our timidity about public praying, even with a friend or small group of friends?

Last year, before the elections in India, Bishop George Isaac from the Church of South India and I had a conversation about the possible impact of the Hindu political party taking a majority of the seats in parliament. The bishop feared that one possible outcome of such elections would be a growing intolerance toward other religions. In fact the bishop said that he had heard some talk about the outlawing of public witnessing of the faiths, which would mean no more public worship or baptisms.

The bishop said that if the government were to ban public profession, he would simply go to the individual families and call on them to become the *misseo dei*, the missional presence of God. "I would encourage them to contact their neighbors," he said, "and make themselves available to pray with them, whenever there was a need for a prayer."

Send the church members to their neighbor, not inviting them to a church service but simply to say, "You know, if you ever face a moment when you would like to have prayer, I'd be glad to pray with you." Offering prayer as a way of outreach seems a simple solution, but with a challenging edge to it.

As I listened to the bishop, I thought about our church here. Prayer is an opportunity for outreach in a simple gesture of kindness. What would it be like if our church members said something similar to their neighbors, "You know, if you ever face a moment when you would like to have prayer, I would be glad to pray with you." Of course, we'd have a lot of work to do to equip most Presbyterians to feel comfortable to lead a prayer with a neighbor or a stranger.

Maybe we could do more praying in this Presbyterian Church we love—more prayers by the laity, encouraged by the clergy, teaching and equipping and sharing in the life of prayer with friends and neighbors. You might ask the Presbytery Council

Editorial

members who are now praying for our congregations each time they meet. Or, ask the Youth Committee members who are now praying for our congregations whenever they hold a meeting.

In January, my council prayer assignment was the Tennessee Church in Teneha, Texas, where I learned about and prayed for a wonderful community of the faith. Averaging twenty in worship most Sundays, this is a congregation of generous givers. In September they raised one thousand dollars for the Florida hurricane relief and later in the fall, they tithed their sixty-thousand dollar savings account to the denomination's Hearts and Hands campaign. A six-thousand-dollar gift from twenty people, who don't worry but simply give. I'd have never learned this if I hadn't picked up the telephone with my prayer assignment in hand.

What place does an active life of prayer play in your vision for your congregation/council? What more can you do to encourage this discipline?

29

Needing One Another

June 2006

From February through May 2006, I was granted a sabbatical leave. I used the time to sail a thirty-one-foot sloop across the Gulf of Mexico, return, and then write about the adventure of meeting fellow sailors, exploring the Yucatan Peninsula, and living simply. It was one of the most profound experiences of my life. This was my report to the presbytery upon my return.

―◇―

Most of you know that my original plans for a twelve-week sailing voyage were curtailed. Due to problems with replacing a mainsail, I ended up spending seven weeks on the water and my final five weeks reading, writing and visiting our children. On our boat, *Azure Wind*, I saw a part of God's world from a very different perspective. I met interesting people. I learned about the challenges of long-distance sailing, life in an anchorage, the culture of northern Mexico. I saw beautiful sunsets, dolphins in the middle of the gulf, the Mayan ruins at Chichen Itza, and joined Sam's Club in Cancun. I visited the church and missed the community of faith I know and need. There are lots of stories and some insights I'd gladly share, but for today, permit me to tell one.

Needing One Another

In the early morning hours of Good Friday, just past midnight, we received a call on the VHF radio. We were on our way back from Isla Mujeres, about six hundred miles into the eight-hundred-mile crossing, heading northwest toward Galveston. The VHF radio is part of the safety net on any boat. You never turn it off even though you seldom hear anything on it. Another crew member was on watch, I was resting below. In the dark, the crew member was tracking two sets of lights on the horizon with a good distance between them. Around 12:30 AM, the radio crackled, "This is the CV *Aquarius* (Commercial Vessel *Aquarius*) trying to reach the small vessel at twenty-eight degrees fifty minutes north and ninety-three degrees fifty-five minutes west, bearing approximately three hundred twenty degrees northwest. I slid out of the quarter berth, grabbed the microphone and identified ourselves as the Sailing Vessel *Azure Wind*. "Yes, Captain, this is *Aquarius* and we have you on our radar moving in the direction of another ship, the CV *Symphony*, which is towing a barge on a three-thousand-meter cable. We advise you to make a course correction and [pause] . . . let me get *Symphony* and you can talk directly. Please stand by."

Azure Wind was heading northwest toward Galveston. *Symphony* was heading northeast toward New Orleans or Mobile. I went up into the cockpit and saw the lights for myself. I had been warned that sometimes barges are towed on long cables, but I never imagined three thousand meters. That's nearly two miles of steel cable. We were on a course that put us crossing behind the first boat and ahead of the second one—the barge. Right into a cable just below or slightly above the water line, a cable that would have broken the keel or taken our mast with a snap.

In minutes, the captain of *Symphony* came on the air and we began the work that saved our lives. Yes, he could see us on his radar. No, we couldn't, our radar was only working at close range. Yes, he could see that our course was taking us into the cable. No, he was not in a position to alter his course. For the next hour, we communicated back and forth. We evaluated our options and then chose to turn on the engine, alter our course, and motor-sail in front of *Symphony*. Finally, when we were past his vessel, *Symphony* called us and we turned back to our original heading.

The myth of self-reliance is pretty well inculcated into the sailing community. The myth says that to be a successful cruiser, you have to not only know how to sail, but you also have to be a diesel mechanic, an electrical engineer, a plumber, carpenter, sailmaker, and in these days, a computer expert. All that may be true, but the rest of the story reminds us of how much we need each other. Three strangers on three ships crossing in the night helped each other. They worked together to keep the seas safe and avoid a catastrophe.

I come back from my time away ever more persuaded that for our church in this time, we desperately need each other. The church is in the midst of a passage from an old world to a new world, from an older way to a newer one. In some ways we are in uncharted, or worse, partially-charted waters. We need each other to make our passages as safe as possible. Even if we're on different vessels, we are wise to appreciate the gifts of faith and perspective others bring, and be willing to work and help each other to keep the church safe and avoid catastrophes. We need each other in our congregations and this presbytery and synod, and our General Assembly and the church ecumenical. We need our liberal and conservative friends, our advocates for change and our advocates for unchanging traditions. We need to help each other listen to God's Word in our time.

Before dawn this past Good Friday morning, as I took the first watch of the day and sat at the helm, I thought about the Navy hymn, *Eternal Father Strong to Save*. The last verse reads:

> O Trinity of love and power, All travelers guard in danger's hour;
>
> From rock and tempest, fire and foe, Protect them wheresoe'er they go;
>
> Thus evermore shall rise to Thee, Glad praise from air and land and sea.

May our prayers include safe passage-making in our lives and may we raise glad praise to God, Three in One, the Trinity of love and power.

The church of Jesus Christ is composed of an interdependent people who are all dependent on God. What can we do to live interdependently?

30

Editorial
Breaking the Silence

July 2006

In 2006, a special work group of the General Assembly made its report. The group was formed by a previous assembly several years earlier and intentionally composed of people reflecting the full diversity of our church. Before the group discussed any of the conflicts we face, the members shared their life and faith stories, learned to pray together, studied the Scriptures in depth and realized that these growing relationships held a pathway forward through the conflicts. The report became a center of attention and contention in 2006.

About the Peace Unity and Purity (PUP) Report:

Finding a way to live together through these stressful times hasn't happened with constitutional amendments. It isn't happening by emphasizing what we hold in common. It is not likely to happen through judicial cases. I say this with much respect for those on the national committee who discovered something true about the church: it takes humility, confession, and listening, to nurture relationships where we can be respected for our beliefs and actions.

Editorial

However, if 43 percent of the commissioners did not agree with the polity part of the PUP report, and if our commissioner selection process reflects something of who we are, then nearly half of our Presbyterian family is hurting right now. Some in mild ways, others in much greater pain. And, it's not simply conservatives who are hurting; there are liberals who are hurting, too. These are the folks who want our church to speak with conviction and clarity about the issues. These are the folks who are on the path of separation.

Here's how that path unfolds. Hurt, followed by silence, leads to anger, followed by silence, leads to balkanization, followed by silence, leads to separation. Something like that.

Some of us inside our congregations are hurting. Others are not. We've probably already talked to our friends, those with whom we share similar opinions. But, if we don't want the path of separation to grab hold any more than it already has, then we'd best do something now: break the silence.

On the day the PUP report was approved, I telephoned one of the pastors who I knew would be deeply disappointed by the assembly's actions. I love this brother in Christ even though we disagree on the challenges facing us. I picked up the phone and said something like, "Friend, I know this report has been of concern to you. I just want to see how you are doing, what you're really thinking and feeling right now." I listened and believe my call was the way Christ would want me to respond.

We ministers, elders, deacons, parishioners have a choice. Keep the silence or break it. If we keep silent, don't be surprised by the anger. If we break the silence, be open to the Spirit of God doing something different in you and others. Sitting back and waiting is not of God right now, not on this matter. Break the silence, please.

All it takes is for one person to break the silence. Who is hurting in your community or leadership team where breaking the silence is God's work for you?

31

Faithful Presence

January 2011

In November 2009, I accepted the invitation to serve as Interim Executive Presbyter in Grand Canyon Presbytery. My reports were often built on previous ones shared in other presbyteries. The key themes from my previous service were shared: the importance of listening, of facing our conflicts, of building of stronger relationships, the Missional Church Initiative, and the opportunity to go exploring and engage this season of change. Occasionally, there was a new insight, including one about the difference between political activism and public witness.

Christians in this country struggle to be clear about the very nature of the church's mission. How are we to live this faith? In what ways are we, born in the image of our creator God, our world-creating God, supposed to be "world creators" ourselves? To this point, we often quote Matthew chapter 28, "Go into all the world making disciples of all nations" (vv. 16–20). We read about those before us who offered the good news in the days of the Reformation, and later colonialism, and understand that the very founding of our nation rests at the hand of a merciful and redemptive God.

But what of us—in this time and place? Is it the church's mission to change the world? Is our mission to redeem the culture?

It is to these questions that a book published last year offers a poignant response. Contrary to those who think that all it takes to change the world is one great leader with the right idea, or one energetic generation of believers committed to a particular set of values, the author of this book, James Davison Hunter, a professor at the University of Virginia, disagrees. The title of his book is *To Change the World: The Irony, Tragedy and Possibility of Christianity in the Late Modern World*. Mr. Hunter fundamentally questions those who think that the way to change our culture is through political action, through legislating values, through heralding particular ideas. That criticism is directed equally to the conservative and the liberal wings of Christianity in this country. Not just Christian conservatives and liberals, but those in the other religions as well.

Consider three of Mr. Hunter's insights:

First, Christians, liberal and conservative, have too simplistic a view of the world and what makes up our culture. Culture is more than simply a set of ideas and how we express them. It is more than our movies and our iPads. Culture is also about people, the people who have influence, the elites of society. It's about the institutions and networks and technologies we use to communicate with one another. Our culture is too complex to think that even the big ideas, such as "freedom" or "justice" can hold us together because our people are too diverse. Our world and our culture are simply too complex to think we have the capacity to change it.

Second, Christians, liberal and conservative, engage the world out of a desire to change all that's wrong with it. It is criticism and negativism that drives action; it is a desire to make perfect God's creation, and behind that is an anger and a resentment that the world isn't the way we think it should be. As such, liberals and conservatives fail to honor the goodness in God's creation, including each other.

Third, Christians, liberal and conservative, have allowed the church's public witness to be reduced to political engagement. Elect the right leaders with the good ideas; change the laws; defend our principles in the courts. That's where we citizens must encounter one another, but we fail in the church if we think that's an effective way to make our Christian witness. Consider the witness, for example, of those who are pro-life. What kind of statement would the church make if say, ten thousand people in the city of Phoenix, signed a pledge stating that they would adopt any child, regardless of race, religion, nationality. Then on the steps of the Maricopa County courthouse they declared there are no unwanted children in Phoenix, Arizona. How different that public witness would be, compared to the political engagement the church has participated in through the years.

In effect, people from James Dobson of Focus on the Family, to Jim Wallis of Sojourners don't get it.

So, what then, is the church's mission? Built on a passage from the 29th chapter of Jeremiah, Hunter says the church is called to engage the world and the culture as those in exile: God instructs the Israelites in Babylon "to seek the welfare of the city where I have sent you." Our mission isn't to change the culture but to engage it. We are to be faithful to God by being a faithful presence in our time and place, nurturing disciples of Jesus Christ and serving the common good.

As Christian citizens, we are quite right to participate in the political processes around us, but the community of faith is to stand as a witness to the loving God whom we know in Jesus Christ by being faithfully present. Faithful presence is a helpful image for the church's mission. It brings together passion, gratitude for God's goodness in the world, humility and respect.

Friends, this is an offensive book, not unlike the gospel itself. Maybe it will push some of us to take another look at what we're doing for the sake of the church's mission.

Is changing the world the Christian community's calling? Where is your leadership team and community engaged in political activism? Where are they engaged in public witness? Is waiting for the right leader the way to live faithfully? Is motivating the people to action the way to live faithfully?

32

Listen More. Laugh Often. Love Always.

November 2013

My final report as Interim Executive Presbyter to Grand Canyon Presbytery ended twenty-five years of mid-council service.

Moderator and Friends:

Thank you for the privilege of serving you and serving God with you these last four years. It has been a great joy for me. And I am grateful for your tolerating the inconvenience from my decision to keep my home in Tucson and commute. I am aware that I was not as present for you as I might have been, but I know that what sanity I have was nurtured by being home as many nights as I was.

I trust my final written report speaks for itself. You have accomplished much these past four years, lived through several important decision moments and now are poised to begin a truly hopeful next step with brothers and sisters in the Presbytery de Cristo.

I am so glad that my formal service has ended here. God's call to me found a home in serving presbyteries, what we now call mid-councils. It became for me a strong passion. Over the course of this past quarter century, I tried to focus on (1) finding solid pastoral leaders for our congregations, (2) helping four mid-councils claim God's leading in these changing times, (3) encouraging honesty and conciliation in times of conflict, and (4) nurturing respect across the spectrum of our theology and practices. Respect, curiosity, and delight in a God who would gather together such a wonderfully diverse people. That has been God's call to me and I look forward to resting in God as I reflect on what I've witnessed in you and the three other presbyteries I've served, and the four hundred congregations with whom I visited and became acquainted.

I leave you with a gift and a charge. Several years ago I learned that when a mother ostrich lays her egg, she never leaves the nest any farther than she can keep one eye on it. She may forage for food, but always within sight of her egg. For the last four years, I have driven by the Rooster Cogburn Ostrich Farm near Picacho Peak, as many as six times in a week. This is your ostrich egg; hang it in the office, bring it to your gatherings.

Let this egg remind you that Grand Canyon Presbytery is giving birth to a new life for this mid-council. By the grace of God, in Jesus Christ and through the Holy Spirit, you are becoming a new community of church leaders, teaching and ruling elders. Always keep one eye on this great and most precious charge.

And to get there, I charge you to do three things:

- Listen more.
- Laugh often.
- Love always.

It would seem that after forty years of a vocational career with twenty-five of them serving mid-councils, one might find something a little more eloquent to offer. But this is it: listen more, laugh often, love always.

Moderator, I've said enough. Be well, friends. God bless you. Go in peace.

33

A Final Thought

No Whining Allowed/Aloud

July 2014

The highest mountain in New Mexico is Wheeler Peak, located in the Taos Ski Valley. Its summit reaches thirteen thousand one hundred feet above sea level. Our family has climbed Wheeler many times over the years. In the 1990s, it was an annual vacation event. The easiest route to the top is a three-mile hike. The first two miles take you from the parking lot at ten thousand feet to eleven thousand. The last mile adds the final two thousand feet, well above the tree line. It's a 40-percent grade! Our youngest daughter, Kate, was eight years old when she made her first climb. Her older brothers, not being very sympathetic to their sister's cries of "How much longer?" took up the mantra, "No whining allowed, Kate." The boys would look back and even before she'd speak, they'd say, "No whining allowed." She wasn't happy, but she kept moving. She made it to the top on her first attempt, and fell in love with Wheeler.

No whining allowed. Once, I was wandering through the General Assembly's Exhibit Hall and found a button that had a red circle and slashing line with one word on it: "Whining." I bought it immediately and it's been pinned to the visor of every truck I've driven since.

Except for the time I sailed across the Gulf of Mexico when I took that button with me, pinned to my knit cap. The eight-hundred-fifty-mile sail was, for me, as challenging and scary an adventure as I've known. On more than one occasion, I needed Kate's button just to keep going.

Sailing has taught me a lot about life and the church. Where I once saw the church as an immovable rock, able to withstand the storms, I now see the church as a boat in constant motion, moving and adjusting to the seas as they change. And as important as the integrity of the boat's construction is to its survival, equally so are the skillful sailors who steer it.

None of us knows exactly where God is leading the church in our country these days. For Presbyterians, we may cheer or agonize over the changes and decisions of our elected commissioners. Regardless, we all face the same seas and go wherever the winds take us. Compared to fifty years ago, we are sailing in rougher seas and none of us can change that fact. For all of the tension among the crew, we would do well to pay a little more attention to the seas around us—what the wind and waves are saying.

No whining allowed, friends! Or if you must, no whining aloud. Follow Christ, stay vigilant, keep the ship moving, and ride this stormy season out.

Appendix A

Parting Thoughts

Going Fast, Going Far

If you want to go fast, go alone; if you want to go far, go together (African proverb). The relationships we have (or don't have) will determine how far we go together.

Building Trust

In new relationships, you build trust by staying spiritually grounded so you don't become anxious when others do. You build trust by making sure all voices invested in a conversation are given the chance to be heard. You build trust by being transparent about your own passions and honest about your mistakes. You build trust by inviting all of us to remember that the church *is* different: God has put us together and we best remember that fact when the pain of our differences may tempt us to jump ship. And God expects us to live in hope, to be passionate and humble in our faith, and to do the right and just thing in our work.

Appendix A

The Authority of the Bible

One of the key ideas of the Reformation is that each Christian has direct access to God, and not through an intermediary, like a priest. We can pray to God. We can read God's word and decide what it means.

One of the patterns I've noticed is that there are a lot of pastors who don't equip their parishioners to read, interpret, and understand the Scriptures. I've also noticed there are a lot of parishioners who don't want to do the work of reading, let alone interpreting, the Scriptures. So, we bemoan the biblical illiteracy of the people, but don't do much about it.

Now that's not true for all pastors. One of them, Rev. Dr. Bill Carl, pastor of First Presbyterian Church, Dallas, taught New Testament Greek for over twenty years. His class was one of the most popular adult education offerings in this large church, so popular that downtown Dallas politicians and professionals—non-members—started attending. Bill was equipping God's people to read the Scriptures for themselves. And this intellectual equipping became a form of outreach.

However, there are too many parishioners in other congregations who shake their Bibles and condemn anyone who has a different interpretation. Too many of them don't know what they're talking about; they are simply quoting their pastors. "The pastor says the Bible says . . . And that's good enough for me." And I suspect there are more than enough pastors who like it this way. So, while the Bible may be the authority for pastors, more often than not, the pastors are the authority for the people.

If we want to equip our people to live according to the Scriptures, pastors might do well to do less telling what the Bible says and more teaching of how to read the Scriptures. Let the people learn by doing the homework, not listening to the pastor's book report.

The Beginning of Conflict

No one is powerless. Therefore everyone involved in any experience in life shares responsibility. Everyone has some power. We use our power both for ourselves (self-interest) and for others (common good). In every experience involving some other person(s), we measure others and ourselves. Is the other exercising power primarily out of self-interest? Is the other making room for me to bring some of my power to this experience? When we experience the other as self-focused, we begin pushing back in order to make room for ourselves and avoid the experience of desperation; we all fear desperation because we understand that desperate creatures take desperate actions. They strike back; they can bring harm to the other.

Anger

My first exposure to rage-aholism was in the 1990s. I suspect I had seen it before, but that word was new to me. The rage-aholic is one who seeks to control others with sudden outburst of anger. You live in fear of being called out, scolded, or shamed, so you tiptoe whenever that person is around so as not to set him/her off.

There once was a pastor who was a loner. He seldom attended the pastors' support group in his area of Eastern Oklahoma Presbytery, and used such bane excuses as he was too busy, and he didn't need the fellowship. He eventually left, rather suddenly. We heard that his last service was on Christmas Eve and that he had refused the offer of a goodbye reception that afternoon, something a bit amazing for a congregation to offer given the day. After the benediction that night, he walked down the aisle, out the door and down the steps to a waiting car, refusing to greet the people. When we heard this, we knew we had a problem. In January, when the Commission on Ministry visited the session, we asked—in small groups—what the session felt the church needed to do next. Every one of those groups said the same thing: "Heal." And then we heard the stories of the pastor's uncontrollable anger—yelling at

Appendix A

elders in session meetings, at parishioners in the grocery store—unpredictably. I ended up making a special trip to North Carolina to confront this pastor in front of his new Presbytery leadership and they made sure he had counseling and mentoring—until he quit and started selling paint.

Lonely, isolated people who become angry are a danger to themselves and others, and not just in the church. Sometimes the anger is expressed actively, sometimes passively.

We all become angry. I've learned it's better to let it out rather than hold it in, sooner rather than later. I've also learned to examine my anger and recognize the reasons (not getting my way, not having the right people agree with me, etc.). Usually, my anger has more to do with me than it has to do with others.

Anger casts a shadow over others and prevents them from participating fully in the body. And rare is the moment when our anger fully represents God's anger and is justified.

Our Visible Expression of Unity

When I was young, it used to bother me that people had different ideas about communion. And those differences became the fuel for our identity and correctness in our theology. These days, I care less and less about that.

Once, at an ecumenical meeting in Geneva, Switzerland, I found myself in a group of Catholic, Anglican, Orthodox and Lutheran Bishops, along with a few of us Reformers. Each day we had communion—in separate rooms (Catholic and Protestant). The purpose of the meeting was ecumenical unity! The irony struck me enough that I remember suggesting that communion not be offered to anyone since we couldn't participate together. The idea fell on deaf ears.

Worse were the General Assemblies where not participating in communion became a form of protest. Most participated and a few did not. Progressives arguing for inclusion of gay and lesbian folks stood outside the worship hall with protest banners and refused to come to the table. Evangelicals, though less visible in their protest, held "alternative" communion services for their own kind. Shame on all of us, I remember thinking.

Then there was the moment at a Presbytery meeting in Texas where a bishop from the Church of South India and I co-celebrated at the table. The meeting that day had included voting on some controversial constitutional amendments and was filled with arguments, some of them rather ugly. I quietly wept and thanked God as I watched every single member of the Presbytery come forward to the table.

You don't go messing with communion. Like our liturgies say, "All who trust in Jesus are welcomed at the table," and that means every one of us, regardless of our particular stripes, needs to receive God's grace, and the Spirit's healing presence at Christ's table. Communion is a sign to the world of our unity in Jesus Christ. And a reminder to ourselves.

Laughter

A man was taking it easy, lying on the grass and looking up at the clouds. He was identifying shapes when he decided to talk to God. "God," he said, "how long is a million years?" God answered, "In my frame of reference, it's about a minute." The man asked, "God, how much is a million dollars?" God answered, "To me, it's a penny." The man then asked, "God, can I have a penny?" God said, "In a minute."

We don't laugh enough in the church. We take our disagreements as life threatening and ourselves too seriously. Laughter is God's way of loosening us up. The Jewish side of my family taught me this. Sitting at the feet of grandparents, uncles, and aunts, I listened to their banter after a meal and began to recognize a people who took faith seriously but themselves much less so. They laughed at their imperfections. They laughed at foolishness, in themselves and others. And they laughed with God. Watching "Fiddler on the Roof," I learned that laughter is like a gentle rain that rinses off the dust, helps us see life more clearly, and teases us into keeping perspective.

Appendix A

There are lots of LOL (laughing out loud) moments in the Scriptures. Abraham and Sarah give birth to Isaac and God laughs. David dances before God's altar and God's clapping keeps time. Maybe the biggest LOL moment of all is Easter Sunday.

God is providential, purposeful, and present. We're part of God's story and need to relax into it. So, what's one extra day? What's one more opinion? What's so special about you that you think you know all the answers anyway?

It would probably help the Presbyterian community if we all took fifteen minutes every day, sitting at our computers, and typed "religious humor" and enjoyed our God a bit more. Besides, our laughter helps us engage the other important matters we face with humility and clarity. If we can be a people who enjoy laughing together, maybe we're not as divided in other matters as we think.

The Drive Was Worth It

In the spring of 1987, we moved from Wausau, Wisconsin, to Kalamazoo, Michigan, and I began what would be a 750,000-mile drive through four presbyteries, four states, and four pickup trucks. I understood the call to serving a presbytery meant a serious commitment to a ministry of visitation, especially on Sunday mornings. Few of us can say that they have visited four hundred Presbyterian churches, most of them more than once. Not one accident I recall, and only a handful of speeding tickets (well, maybe two handfuls!).

In the beginning, most churches welcomed me, asked me to teach an adult class, and often held a potluck lunch on the occasion of a visit. I only preached for special occasions (think building dedication) or emergencies, never as a vacation substitute. In the early years, I sat with the pastor, usually robed, and there was a sense that my presence reflected the presence of the larger church. I was seen as a representative of the mission of the PCUSA. In later years, with the church's increased embattlement over theological ideas and ministry practices, I was seen as a representative of the church's "positions" and welcomed accordingly. That led me to wonder about the value of all that visiting.

On the other hand, there has never been a question about the gift those visits gave to me. I have seen the church in the full breadth of its diversity: large/small, urban/rural, single cultures/many cultures, orthodox/progressive/middle-of-the-road. And I discovered something good about each congregation I visited, even after witnessing some unusual practices. Like the east Texas church that collected the offering before the call to worship, counted the collection on the communion table in front of the congregation and wrote down the total on the chalkboard, next to the day's hymn numbers! That same church had a wonderful children's choir who surely brought joy to the Lord! God changes you when you have a chance to see the breadth of this church.

And I realized that part of my job has been to be a witness to all of you—about the good work God does in large congregations, small ones, too; in urban churches and the most rural, back country, down-the-dirt-road ones; in black, Anglo, Asian, Hispanic, Native, and many-cultured congregations; in the progressive, evangelical, middle-of-the-road, both liberal and conservative communities of believers. I am a witness to amazing worship, amazing mission, amazing fellowship, amazing service.

Something good . . . and godly . . . everywhere. Period. Even as my trucks and body started to slow a bit, there was never a question that the drive was worth it.

The Death of Christianity

"Christianity has died many times and risen again, for it had a God who knew the way out of the grave" (G. K. Chesterton).

The Millennium Resolution

>Let there be respect for the earth,
>Peace for its people,
>Love in our lives,

Appendix A

> Delight in the good,
> Forgiveness for past wrongs,
> And from now on a new start

—composed by the Millennium Group of the Churches Together in England so that Christians, members of other faith communities and people with no faith could join together in a moment of shared reflection (used during England's Millennial Moment just before midnight 12/31/99)

Appendix B
For Further Reflection

Meditation: "Doing Wilderness Work," preached to Eastern Oklahoma Presbytery in March 1997, based on Mark 2:9–15

I wish to begin by offering a bit of perspective. First, it's our turn. Today this presbytery will engage in a conversation, a debate and a vote on several amendments to our constitution. So far, 113 other presbyteries have had their turn. We're not alone today; three other presbyteries are taking their turn, too. It's not only our turn to debate and vote, it's our turn to do this in good Presbyterian fashion: decently and in order. The whole church is watching and expects nothing less than civil, respectful, thoughtful, orderly discourse. Frankly, it's not just the whole church, it's the whole world that's watching because frankly, most of the rest of the world can't do what we're about to do: take our turn at civil and respectful debate.

Second, we're all elders. If you have the privilege of casting a vote on any of the decisions we will make today, whether it's about the proposed amendments or who will be a member of this presbytery, you are an elder of the church. And despite what the world may say, or what most of the attitudes in our congregations convey, you have been given an honor and an important responsibility.

And what elders need to bring with them are three things: manners, intelligence, and courage. The manners that respect the dignity of others, the intelligence that stands at the heart of our tradition, and the courage to stand for what may be unpopular. And again, that places you at odds with the world, for most of the world's leaders lack at least one, if not more, of these: manners, intelligence, courage.

Third, we've been here before. Underlying much of this church's struggle in recent years is the age-old question: What shall be the marks of the true church? Righteousness? Grace? In one of the first of the ancient church's controversies, righteousness was the mark. The congregations were admitting those Christians who had burned incense before the Roman gods, individuals who were judged to have lost the mark of holiness. Two centuries later, it was grace. When some in the church were calling those who had turned over the Scriptures to the Roman "traitors," Bishop Augustine would not exclude them. Charity and grace are the true marks of the church he wrote. So, in our time, we face this old question once more: What shall be the marks of the true Church? Righteousness? Grace? Peace? Unity? Purity?

Four, there are other pressing matters. Theological and moral debates are a luxury of sorts. We make them into necessities, but let's be serious. There's a country out there that's waiting for the Presbyterian Church and its congregations to proclaim God's good news in ways that turn peoples' heads and hearts and lives around. It is a country that is divided by racism while it continues to grow racial enclaves. It is a country divided by economics as it continues to grow the gap between rich and poor. Our country needs a church that knows how to build bridges to all God's people. Frankly, the people who are drinking foul water and scrambling to grab at the few morsels of bread left over from the tables of the rich, and those who are crying "injustice" from prison cells, . . . these people aren't interested in our ecclesiastical constitution. *We* need to be, but we also need to remember that there are other issues that call to us and press upon us as we dare to live the faith of one John of Patmos, who wrote: "God so loved the world that he gave his only

For Further Reflection

Son, so that everyone who believes in him may not perish but may have eternal life" (John 3:16).

Perspective. It's all a matter of perspective.

And to all of this, I sense God's Word comes from the opening chapter of Mark's gospel:

> In those days Jesus came from Nazareth of Galilee and was baptized by John in the Jordan. And just as he was coming up out of the water, he saw the heavens torn apart and the Spirit descending like a dove on him. And a voice came from heaven, "You are my Son, the Beloved; with you I am well pleased." And the Spirit immediately drove him out into the wilderness. He was in the wilderness forty days, tempted by Satan; and he was with the wild beasts; and the angels waited on him. (Mark 1:9–13)

Where Matthew and Luke provide details of both Jesus' baptism and temptation, Mark gives us the broad sweep of the beginning of our Lord's ministry in but a few words.

Three weeks ago, the lectionary drew our attention to this passage. Three weeks later, there are two afterthoughts. First, after baptism there is temptation. I'm sure Mark was simply recording the sequence of events, but I'd humbly suggest that God wants us to remember that baptism is no panacea for an easy life. Once we claim in our baptism the love God has already claimed in Christ, we are not immune to difficulties and hardships and irritations and pain-in-the-you-know-what days. And I know we all know this because I suspect every preacher here has preached his or her version of it and every elder here understands how hard the real world can be. And yet, the temptation that's hard to resist is the temptation to resent those who make life hard for me or you. The people I disagree with and who just don't get "it" and can't understand why what I think is so important and there must be something wrong with them to think the way they do and it just irritates me no end that I have to put up with someone or several ones like that. God, I thought you did promise a rose garden and my life was going to be easy and don't tell me that these people who make my life hard could possibly have anything to do with you. After baptism the temptations come and among them in this season of the church's life is the one that says you have no right to make my life difficult. So, cut it out . . . Well, *excu-u-u-use* me, for just one moment. The difficult moments of my life and your life, and the troubling, frustrating moments of the church's life may be exactly what God wants right now, and we do well to resist the resentment toward those who irritate our life's landscape.

The second afterthought to this passage is this. After baptism, we start to hear voices from heaven. We may not literally hear a voice from afar, but when we take our baptism seriously we begin the hard work of listening for God's voice and God's leading, living the faith and being part of the church. It means declaring, of all things, that God alone is Lord of the conscience which is not some excuse for the rampant individualism and growing congregationalism such as the likes we are seeing in this country these days. That God alone is Lord of the conscience means that the work of naming and proclaiming the love of God or even the best way to phrase the constitution of the church begins with your conscience and my conscience, your integrity and my integrity, your heart and my heart. It may mean the freedom to stand alone which is not the same as standing apart, as though somehow we have the option to disconnect from the rest of the body. We listen for the voice of God, and when we think we hear it we are driven into our own kind of wilderness, which for Presbyterians isn't so much of a lonely place as it is a noisy place. And the real temptation is that we want to get to the noisy place where we all take our turn speaking before we go to the quiet place of the listening heart and mind. The temptation is to come to moments like today and think we have done all our listening and thinking and we now have God's truth solely in our possession and God's voice solely resonating from our words, and of course that's usually when God plays a little trick on us. Just when we think we have it all figured out and just when we think we know what's best for the church, just at the moment when we cross the line between passion to arrogance, that's often when God does something that catches our attention and humbles us and reminds us just who is in charge of all of this. We are reminded that it is at

For Further Reflection

God's feet we can in confidence lay our heart's and mind's matters, and trust that good will prevail. If you don't believe me, just ask old patriarch Jacob after a night at the Jabbok, or just ask old King David after a word with Nathan, or just ask Paul after a blinding moment on the road to Tarsis, look inside and just ask yourself.

The temptation, I think is to forget to put on the mantle of humility, and to consider that maybe we haven't done enough wilderness work yet. Maybe there's more discerning and listening and praying and thinking and sharing of ourselves ahead, and just maybe we don't have it exactly as God has it, or God would have it for us. Maybe.

So, we gather as an expression of that wonderfully diverse part of the body of Christ that calls itself Presbyterian. We gather to do a little wilderness work, some of it quietly and some of it noisily, I suspect. Somewhere down the course of this day, some of us are going to be tempted to feel elation and others to feel disappointment. Even so, God's angels will wait upon all of us, if we all present ourselves as true elders, with manners, intelligence and courage, and if we all wrap ourselves in the humility of the saints. May God stand with us and hold us close.

Amen.

Appendix B

Sermon: "Purgatory Café," preached to Grace (Texas) Presbytery in September 2002, based on John 15:1–17

"I am the true vine, and my Father is the vinegrower" (v. 1).

Several years ago, I came across a one-act play by the name of *Café Purgatory*, written by John Wooley. It was performed off Broadway, as in west of the Hudson River; well, off, off Broadway, as in west of the Mississippi; well, actually in Tulsa. There's only one scene: a cafe setting with a counter and stools, and a few tables and chairs, and a door leading to the outside. The story begins with a young woman and a middle-aged couple entering the cafe, having awakened from the last thing they remember—their deaths in an automobile accident. They discover that the cafe is the waiting place, where people who die come and wait for what happens next. The cafe proprietors then reveal the premise of the story: you can't leave the cafe until those on earth who knew you accept your death. Once that happens, then you can step through the door and claim your eternal reward or . . . not. In the midst of their conversation, the characters notice a middle-aged man sitting on a barstool, head resting on the counter—asleep and dressed in a white jumpsuit. The proprietor explains that it's a sad case—a man who's been in the cafe for twenty-five years, just waiting for the people on earth to accept the fact that he's dead. The couple look closer and realize they know him. It's Elvis—stuck in purgatory cafe because there are still some folks who think he's alive. It's a fun little play and the cafe serves up an interesting premise.

"I am the true vine, Jesus says, and my Father is the vinegrower" (v. 1).

Purgatory Cafe is not very defensible as a theology, but friends, there's a sense in which the church that you and I have known growing up is stuck in purgatory cafe. That church has died, and it's time to let it go. We know this old church in a variety of ways. Some of us harken back to the 1950s, where we grew congregations the same way some folks grow those prized vegetables for the state fair. Others of us talk about the old successes of Westminster Fellowship groups and the Christian Faith in Action curricula and long for the time when it all made sense and we all worked together in common cause from the local church to the General Assembly. We recall with pride our mission story: from those early colonial beginnings and our contributions to establishing a constitutional government, to our posture toward westward expansion and insisting on educated pastors; from the ways we embraced the emerging urban life of our cities, to the post–World War II churches of the suburbs and shopping malls. We want to believe that the age of Christendom is still alive—that the church *can still* shape the political character and culture without being distorted by it. And we don't want to admit that that old church has died, or at the very best is an ICU patient being held together by the life support systems of some types of endowment funds, low paid clergy and entrenched attitudes about our worship, music, Scripture and learning.

"He removes every branch in me that bears no fruit. Every branch that bears fruit he prunes to make it bear more fruit" (v. 2).

For all the good that the church of Christendom has brought, it is not going to be the way of the twenty-first-century church. And the fact is, in some ways the Christendom church has not done very well. The declining membership of mainline denominations is just one indicator. When we survey ourselves we see other indicators. We discover that Jesus' disciples who sit in our pews aren't getting it. Two out of three pew sitters don't encourage others to believe in Jesus Christ. Five out of ten don't give their time to help the poor. Six of ten don't engage in daily prayer. Six in ten don't read the Bible when alone. Less and less, we see the authority of Jesus in the church we've built. Too often we find ourselves working hard to work around this institutional church that we worked hard to create in the first place. Membership in a congregation carries with it few serious expectations. And from several meetings with our ministers these last few months, I'm learning that we clergy want a presbytery to expect of us about as much as our churches expect of its members. The authority of the church no longer reflects the authority of Christ, to us within it, or to the world outside. A news release in July says it all: public confidence in US religious institutions is at a thirty-year low. Last year 60 percent of Americans said they had confidence in the church, synagogue, and mosque. Today it's 45 percent. Churches and organized religion rank sixth in public confidence, behind the military, the police, the presidency, the Supreme Court and banks. And the scandal in the Catholic Church only partly explains this dramatic shift.

"Abide in me as I abide in you. Just as the branch cannot bear fruit by itself unless it abides in the vine, neither can you unless you abide in me. I am the vine, you are the branches" (v. 4–5).

Folks, the church of Christendom is slumped on a barstool in purgatory cafe, waiting for the last person on earth to admit that this old church has died. We're finally de-constructing an old church that barely exists, and admitting the ways we've been cut off from Christ the true vine. And at the same time the winds of the Spirit are blowing, and here and there we're beginning to construct a new church for the twenty-first century. Something new is calling to us, but we're not going to get there until we let go of some old assumptions, let go of some old ways of building the church, and do so in spite of a few people who won't.

"If you abide in me, Jesus says, and my words abide in you, ask for whatever you wish, and it will be done for you. My Father is glorified by this, that you bear much fruit and become my disciples" (vv. 7–8).

What will the twenty-first-century church look like? What will it emphasize? In this moment, we still see in a mirror dimly. Even so, I see a new church emerging that will be more honest about not confusing God's mission with the church's. Institutional survival is not God's mission; making disciples and sending apostles is. God's kingdom comes to earth first through disciples and apostles, and not through a denominationalized faith. We are called to become disciples and to bear fruit as apostles. And the fruit we bear that's worthy of God's harvest is simply the good works done in union with Christ. Make disciples and send apostles. That's the mission of God in this world and the call today to every congregation and

For Further Reflection

to every presbytery and synod and our General Assembly is simply this.

"As the Father has loved me, Jesus told his disciples, so I have loved you; abide in my love. If you keep my commandments, you will abide in my love. This is my commandment, that you love one another as I have loved you" (vv. 9–10).

The twenty-first-century church will also act differently about being the church. It will have a different ecclesiology. Nearly ten years ago, Jack Stotts, now retired president from two of our seminaries and chair of the committee that gave us the last entry into our Book of Confessions, the Brief Statement of Faith, wrote an interesting paper about the nature of the church. In it he identifies four different models of being the church, based on four different Old Testament images: the exodus, the exile, the time of the judges, and the Davidic kingdom. For instance, the church for some is imagined as an ongoing exodus, bringing poor and captive people to liberation and freedom, calling for a rebalancing of social, political and economic power. The church has also been fashioned after the exile, seeing itself in a strange land, singing a new song, bemoaning the loss of Christian values in the culture. Some look to the time of the judges in building the church, creating independent local communities of worship and nurture that have only a vague idea that they're part of a mission larger than themselves. And still others look to the time of King David, where to some degree like Calvin, they imagine Christendom and want to elevate the church to a position of power over all arenas of life. Authority is centralized or decentralized in these various models, but none, says Stotts, is sufficiently able to create a church for the future. The love of Christ must be at the center of the twenty-first-century church. Sounds simple, but it's not because Jesus isn't talking about *agape*—he's talking about *philia*.

"I do not call you servants any longer, because the servant does not know what the master is doing; but I have called you friends" (v. 15).

The journey we disciples make with Jesus is complex, isn't it? Our relationship often begins as teacher-student. He is rabbi, the one with the good ideas that are worth following. But then we realize that's not enough. We become servants to a master, a Lord, to the one who has the power over our lives because we give it to him. We will obey, even if we don't fully get the picture. We obey because he is Lord. And then, at the last supper, Jesus tells us that we're now friends. I think some of us get stuck at this part. We either sentimentalize a friendship with Jesus, or we can't imagine a relationship with Christ that reflects the character of a deep friendship, qualities that include intimacy and mutuality, according to Stotts. I've now reached an age where I'm grateful to say I have a friend of nearly fifty years. My kindergarten classmate and I have shared a first communion, tossed graduation caps, stood at each other's weddings, set tent poles, and even hauled sailing lines. He's a deep friend and the words "intimate" and "mutual" describe the love we share. The love of Christ as friend is not like two people standing face to face, but rather like two people standing side by side, because they both can see where they're headed. *I have called you friends because I have made known to you everything that I have heard from my Father.* Friends who walk together, work together, sing together, cry together, laugh together. It takes time, attention, and effort to build this kind of friendship, whether it is with a best friend or with Christ the Lord who calls us a friend.

"You did not choose me but I chose you. And I appointed you to go and bear fruit, fruit that will last" (vv. 16–17).

We who are beginning to construct an ecclesiology for the twenty-first-century church do well to take these words of Jesus to heart. Church order in the future is going to be built less on power and more on mutual accountability, less on rules and more on relationships, more on Jesus as Friend. The tightly woven existence of a church based on power from governing bodies, a thicker Book of Order and judicial challenges of our constitution is unraveling before our eyes. Bishops, whether they are individuals or groups such as a presbytery, are increasingly irrelevant. They have less and less authority, and people are inclined to ignore them or sue them or defy the constitutions they represent. They have less and less authority because they have been failing to invest themselves in

For Further Reflection

the labor intensive work of building relationships: building friendships of mutuality and intimacy and respect, building friendships that lead to a different kind of accountability than one based on power and hierarchy. To suggest that the twenty-first-century church needs to be grounded in Christ as Friend is to suggest more than looking for the presence of Christ in the people around us, in "those" people with whom disagree or dismiss, even though this would surely help. It calls for a church, congregations and presbyteries included, where people invest in the labor-intensive work of setting aside ourselves to meet others where they are: of being less concerned to announce the Christ in us than to respond to the Christ in the other, of being friends who walk side by side because they share the Christ-given vision of discipleship and apostleship; friends who can't fix the other's problems as much as they can stand with them in their moments of trial; friends who do have expectations of each other but who grieve more than they punish when those expectations aren't met. In such a church, we understand that we don't choose each other any more than we choose Christ. Christ chooses us and appoints us to go and bear fruit. And we're not going to do that without first investing ourselves in the work of deep friendship, as hard, and time-consuming, and frustrating as it can sometimes be. Such work, building a church on Christ as Friend, just might open the door of our café purgatory, and take us into the future God has in store for us.

As we prepare to gather around the table of our Lord, this passage invites us to come to the table not as students, not as servants, but as friends, where in the breaking of bread and in the sharing of the cup we allow ourselves to be nourished by our friendship with Christ and our friendship in Christ with each other. Christ has called each of us friends. Can we do anything less with each other? So we are invited to this table. And so we are called to leave the table to do the work of ministry, as Christ's friends and friends in Christ. Thank God.

Amen.

Appendix B

Sermon: "Mishpat. Hesed. Humble Walking," preached to Grace Presbytery in November 2006, based on Micah 6:1–8 and Luke 4:16–21

Opening Words: *On October 2nd, a deranged, distraught father entered a schoolhouse and murdered five innocent girls before taking his own life. For a few days, we looked upon a way of life that is foreign to almost all of us. What we found inside the Amish community in the midst of deep sorrow, was not revenge or anger, but compassion. The Amish pointed to Jesus and gave us a reminder that religion need not turn lethal or combative.*

Faced with important issues though far less sinister, including our divisions over sin and obedience, and ordination, people, mostly inside the Presbyterian Church and some outside, are watching to see if we can lead with repentance, forgiveness, grace, and without hostility. And to walk the walk of Jesus, we need God's help. Pray for God's help.

Let's remember a couple of things as we begin.

First, most of us will let someone be a truth-teller to us. For some, it's the spouse who can tell us where we're messing up, or a brother or sister or close friend. For others, it's an authority figure: a supervisor at work, or a teacher at school. And for some, it's the Word of God that can bare our souls. Most of us go kicking and screaming, resisting and resenting these moments of naked truth-telling. Even so, most of us will trust some "other" enough to listen and consider that maybe, just maybe, we've blown it in some way, be it a piece of our personal lives, or a piece of our church life.

Second, confession and truth-telling are not easy. They usually come with a cost, the most basic of which is that we will have to *change* something about the way we live, or in our case this evening, the way we lead. It's no wonder that confession in our worship all too often seems hollow, rote, less than heartfelt. Those words we read on the piece of paper in front of us seldom bring us to our knees in a terrible realization that, "O my God, I haven't been doing enough; I do the things I know I shouldn't; I don't lead in a way that I know I should." That kind of confession we avoid like a plague.

Third, about the texts: let's remember that Micah and Isaiah were contemporaries, both prophets speaking to a people and a nation in serious trouble. The kingdom of Israel to the north had already been destroyed. And Judah was no better off. There are exegetical questions about both books, about authorship, and even passages where both prophets are quoting the same words. For tonight that is not so important.

More important is the question that Micah answers: "Just what kind of God do we serve, what does God expect of us?" Micah reminds us that this is the God of the exodus and Mt. Sinai: of rescue and of covenantal law, of deliverance and grace. And in our response, we must not confuse our worship, our sacrifice, our adoration with appeasement, when all God wants is reconciliation, our trust, honor and faithfulness. These, by the way, are a heck of a lot easier to offer than *appeasement*, because when you try to appease God, you can never be really sure that your response, your pledge, your prayers will be enough. It's that old competitive thing between Cain and Abel. Whose burnt offering, whose gift, satisfies God more? That's not what God expects of us, trumpets Micah.

Rather, God wants a sacrifice of practicing justice, *mishpat*, which goes beyond the limits of the law to rectifying the inequities of a society. God wants a sacrifice from lawmakers and power grabbers who do the oppressing and deny basic needs to some and prevent them from functioning as part of the community. God wants mishpat, and God wants *hesed*: to love mercy, to be faithful to the covenant, compassionate, offering steadfast love. God wants a sacrifice where we live with one another in community the way God has lived toward us, with hesed. And God expects us to walk humbly, to walk the path of a godly lifestyle, to live by rejecting self-centeredness and to listen to God through our prayers, reflections and through the people who cross our path in life, including others in the church. Mishpat, hesed, walk humbly. That's what God expects.

Appendix B

If there was ever an ordination question worth adding to that excruciatingly long list of constitutional questions we ask of our church leaders, it would be this: Do you promise to do justice, to love kindness, and to walk humbly with our God?

So in walks Jesus to the cathedral which, according to Luke, is the third act of his public ministry. He's been baptized, he's been tempted, and then he declares his mission. His mission isn't to make disciples, not really. *His* mission is to show the way to God, to allow the curious to get close enough to ask about being a follower and then show them what it will require of them: do justice and love mercy, or as Isaiah put it, to bring good news to the poor, release to the captives. You know the rest: to proclaim that right now is the acceptable moment of the Lord. It's the acceptable time to repent, to turn around, to face the truth, the hard realities, and to change, to get on with mishpat, hesed, and humble walking.

Tonight is about leadership, your leadership and my leadership in this church. It's about taking this year's themes of call, covenant and community one more step. It's about claiming what it *will* take to lead people of faith all called by God, all agreeing to God's covenant, and all placed in communities to live out their part of the covenant in Jesus Christ. To live it out, we need leaders who get it. Can *we* lead, respecting the call God has given to each person, keep covenant faithfulness, and live in community as though the life of the world depended on it?

One story: At a meeting after this year's General Assembly, we were asked to reflect on the question of "Why Stay?" Why stick around the PCUSA when life, and maybe faith, would be easier if we could just get away from a group of people who don't look, act, think and believe all alike and apparently, at least according to the news media, know how to shoot themselves in the foot *way too much*? Like the people of Judah, our church is in trouble. Numbers alone show enough of a truth that best not be ignored. Put it in your own words, but these aren't bad: we seem to think we can appease God with our sacrifices, our worship, our service, our arguments, and Christ seems to be ready to wipe the dust off his

For Further Reflection

sandals and move on. So rather than ask, "Why Stay?" we might consider, "What will the Lord require of me to stay?"

What is the Lord requiring of us if we want to stay in the Presbyterian Church? Three things, among many. First, fairly basic: *Get used to the diversity in the Presbyterian family*. Get comfortable with being uncomfortable, as General Assembly moderator Joan Gray puts it. This part of the body of Jesus Christ *is* diverse. Maybe we're more diverse than some other parts of Christ's body where the folks apparently look, act, think, and believe in lockstep uniformity. But that's not what God has assembled here. Unless you want to go down the road of suspecting that the people who don't see the Bible the way you do are of the devil, then we'd best show a little respect that we all are trying to be faithful disciples of Jesus Christ. We all are people who think and act about faith and life according to the Protestant and Reformed understandings of God's providence, redemption, and hope. God has put us together, God has assembled us *in our diversity*, frankly to keep us humble. So, get used to it. It's kind of like that Easter bumper sticker that reads: "Christ is risen! Adjust."

Second, for you and me to stay in the Presbyterian Church, God is requiring us *to use some of our time to engage the people who are different than ourselves—to engage this diverse Presbyterian crowd*. Our history is filled with stories of such engagements. And most of them aren't pretty or a source of pride. Liberals and conservatives, "personal salvation-ists" and "social justice-ites" have played too much on the battlefield of victorious defeats. Frankly, there's a younger generation who are fed up with us. They understand diversity, they understand tolerance, and they want to see the Bible and godly behavior brought to this time in which we live. But we've lobbed the missiles of winners and losers, with constitutional amendments trying to draw legislative boundaries that would force some agreement. This year, with an Authoritative Interpretation, we're playing the same game, now arguing over how to interpret a paragraph of some two hundred words. We've built fortresses with our diversity. That's the shameful, naked confession. We have to respectfully get to know the people in our church who are different than ourselves. As uncomfortable as that may make you feel, you are not exempt. So how would you like to spend your time in this engagement? Spend it in more amendment-arguing, or in Bible study? In arguing over what the authoritative interpretation really says, or in prayer and conversation? Like those wristbands, I bet I know what Jesus would do. What does the Lord require of us? *Know and love our diverse family—as people, as human beings, as children of the faith.*

Finally, and frankly most importantly, to stay in the Presbyterian Church God expects us *to stay focused on our primary mission*: helping each other do God's work of justice and witness, service and testifying, of preaching and living as faithfully to God's lifestyle as each of us knows how. To stay focused, to help each other build up a church where the Word of God is rightly preached, the sacraments are rightly administered, the discipline and the whole of mission is rightly upheld. God expects us to invest the majority of our time in worship, prayer, study, service, fellowship, encouragement, and to take our faith into the church-place, the home-place, the marketplace, the school-place, every place. To make each day part of this time when it is acceptable to confess, to turn around, to face the truth, to change and to get on with mishpat, hesed, and humble walking. What truly matters more than anything else? God's work.

For me, the best gift of our General Assembly's Peace, Unity and Purity Task Group report is this word: get comfortable, get engaged, get on with God's work. It's a daunting message because some can't recognize God as the author of our diversity, some don't want to waste their time getting to know people who are different. They want to talk but don't want to listen, and some only want to talk about winning their church battles. But you know what? As leaders in the Presbyterian Church (USA), in this time, those aren't options: Mishpat. Hesed. Humble walking. That's the way given to us.

Mishpat. Hesed. Humble walking. That's the way to approach this table, of our Lord, who is the Prince of Peace.

FOR FURTHER REFLECTION

Mishpat. Hesed. Humble walking. That's the way to approach each other, in the name of our Prince of Peace, Jesus Christ. May the peace of the Lord Jesus Christ be with you . . . In the name of Christ, now go and greet one another.

Amen.